TH💡NK
—A—
BETTER
THOUGHT™

TRAINING YOUR MIND
FOR SUCCESS 101

BY SHANE DUKE BORING

TABLE OF CONTENTS

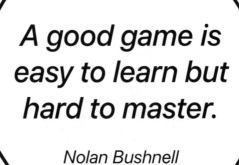

A good game is easy to learn but hard to master.

Nolan Bushnell

CHAPTER 1

SEEKING AND FINDING THE TRUTH

"Are you ever going to be satisfied? Are you ever going to be happy?" My wife, Dedee, used to ask me these questions regularly...for over 20 years!

"What are you talking about?" I'd respond to her. "I'm happy."

She'd look at me, doubtful.

"Besides," I'd add, "Why would I ever want to be satisfied? I'm always striving."

"I just don't think you ever have a moment of peace. You don't actually enjoy anything."

As I now see so clearly, she was right.

I thought my life was supposed to be all about the hustle. I looked at everything in life as a competition - money, relationships, experiences, possessions...everything.

I existed in a mostly unsatisfied state, selfishly feeling short changed and wanting more from every experience I had. I didn't have any comprehension that life is meant to be enjoyed fully.

When Dedee would point out something she appreciated, like a heart-warming story, I would usually think to myself, "Why do I care? How does this story about someone I don't even know help me?" Or, if we achieved a big business goal, my sights would immediately be set upon the next hurdle to overcome, rather than savoring the success in the moment. There was never enough for me.

My greatest problem during this period of my life was that I believed I was 100% right.

I had no idea how isolated, limited, and disconnected my life was. When things went wrong...and they often did, I placed blame on everything and everyone else, especially God.

I wanted God to solve my problems, but I was also terribly afraid of Him judging and punishing me. This practice of placing blame on God for my problems further developed an unhealthy fear that started in my childhood.

I grew up in Wheeler, Texas, a small town just over a thousand in population, sitting right on the edge of the Bible Belt, but it might as well have been in the middle. There wasn't much to do as a kid except go to football games and church, and at least once a year, there would be a revival or big church program that would attract most of the town.

These events were packed with music and emotional preaching about sinners burning in hell for eternity because they were not saved by Jesus. The message I received at these events was that I was a sinner, doomed to death and an eternal punishment. The preachers said my only hope was to be saved by Jesus.

Every event concluded with an altar call. If you're not familiar with an altar call, I'll give you a short description.

An altar call is an invitation to publicly make a spiritual commitment to Jesus Christ. Participants usually leave their seats and meet the priest or a church leader at the altar or in front of the seated congregation. There you are publicly guided to pray and ask Jesus Christ into your life. The promise is that when you do this all your sins are forgiven, and you are assured to live for eternity in Heaven with Jesus.

Think about this for just a second. You're a young child learning about every possible way to go to hell. Adults have spent the last three hours not just scaring the hell out of you but creating a personal hell all around you. And now...you can escape and be saved from this terrifying future just by coming up and praying with someone? Sign me up.

I was saved a lot as a kid...and even a few times as an adult.

I've been saved several, possibly even 10 times. Each time, I was full of energy and feeling good, but that feeling didn't last — something was still missing. This doesn't mean I've never believed in God. I just didn't get the feeling that anything had really changed in my life.

Doomed at 10

A major life event happened to me when I was 10, and in one day I went from going to Heaven to spending an eternity in hell.

I was a victim of sexual abuse. The abuse only happened one time, but I kept the memory of it present with me all the time for many years to come. I didn't see myself as a victim. I saw myself as the ultimate sinner.

Was this the wrong conception of myself? Yes, without any doubt, this was the wrong conception, but it was the only one I had. It was a destructive conception I kept locked away deep inside my inner being.

I saw no way of recovering from it and receiving forgiveness from God.

I feared an eternal punishment in hell after the sexual abuse because I felt like I was the one at fault.

I knew in my young 10-year old mind that I was guilty. Guilt is what I had been taught in my culture.

I lived with guilt, shame, and judgment on a daily basis. I hoped that there was something I could do to get out of it, but I had no idea what that could even be. I didn't ask anyone what they thought because then they would know my deepest, darkest secret. My young mind was overwhelmed with the dark future ahead.

I chose not to say anything about the abuse to anyone. I kept it all inside. This choice helped construct obstacles between me and happiness for over 30 years. There was always that event in the back of my mind that canceled out everything good I could do.

A preview of hell

I accidentally caught my pajama shirt on fire when I was five. I had a half-dollar-size, second-degree burn in the middle of my chest. It was a very small incident, but also very scary and painful.

My only conception of an eternal punishment in hell was to go back to how painful the experience of the small burn on my chest was. I was terrified. All I could imagine was that feeling, amplified all over my body, as a possibility for eternity.

I asked myself over and over, "What kind of God could allow this? Why should I even trust God? If I'm going to burn in Hell for eternity, what's the point in following rules anymore? I'm doomed."

As an adult I continued to have experiences that just didn't add up.

Dedee and I signed up for a class called, Alpha, which was given through the Episcopal church we were attending. The purpose of the class was to help you have a deeper, personal relationship with God, and occurred one evening each week over a 13 week period.

We were close to the end of the course, and were going to finish with a longer, weekend session. This weekend session was focused on the Holy Spirit.

The video we watched in the morning was very inspiring, and the preacher finished strongly with great enthusiasm, claiming that, "If you ask the Holy Spirit to come into your life, you better be ready, because when you ask the Holy Spirit to come in, it won't just come in, it will consume you! You will be overwhelmed with God's power and love. It will come to and through you with great intensity!"

The preacher was more than convincing. I believed every word he was saying.

Immediately, I wanted to experience what the preacher was promising. Why hadn't I been able to experience this before? I was a Christian.

10

Surely, I qualified for this incredible experience.

I was ready to feel the Holy Spirit. I quickly found a room where no one would interrupt me. I just knew that the lights were going to flicker, the wind would be rushing, and that the ground might shake. I thought I might even walk out of the room glowing.

Feeling inspired, looking in the mirror, I intensely invited the Holy Spirit to come saying to myself, "Holy Spirit, come! I am ready to receive you in my life!"

Nothing came. No wind. No vibrating ground. Not even a rattle. Just nothing.

So, I gave it another shot. "Holy Spirit, come! I am ready to receive you in my life!"

Still nothing. What a complete disappointment.

The class lost all its credibility with me. I felt like I had been set up. A class that I believed was helping me gain a closer understanding of God became just another spiritual tool that didn't work.

You may have had similar or different experiences when it comes to seeking real knowledge on how you can gain an understanding of God or how to make your life better. Mine mostly have left me more than a little disappointed, because I've always been an all-in guy.

Whether it was for a workout, business training, or even aiming for sales goals, I'd have the approach, "Let's go as hard as we can. Let's add more! Let's go for it." And, when it came to these experiences with spirituality, I never realized the knowingness of, "Finally, yes, this is right. This is the Truth," that the preachers had been promising me.

I was stuck in this pain of thinking that everyone was making this stuff up. Eventually, I became lazy and quit searching for the answers. I just kept going through the motions, thinking I must be pre-destined for mediocrity, all the while feeling numb on the inside.

There was no way that this was how my life was supposed to be, but it was also the only definition of life I had. I felt cheated, like the game had been set up for me to fail.

The truth is that many of us experience an event that completely changes our outlook on life. Self-inflicted or not, we all have our "junk". It is part of the human experience.

"But my junk is worse. You don't understand." Does this reasoning sound and feel familiar?

I allowed events like my sexual abuse define who I was. I lived with a shadow always hanging over me. I used the sexual abuse as a reason, an excuse, for failure and misfortune. Keeping this event alive limited all the good that had always been available to me.

I felt like my "junk" was just too big to be removed or fixed. I let the little voice inside my head keep me locked inside my own prison of fear and frustration, frequently playing the recordings of my failures over, and over, and over.

I wasn't tuned in. I didn't know who to turn to or where to go. I didn't trust anyone. I was in a constant spiritual funk.

It would take me many more years to discover that the answer for living a spiritually funk free life has always been within me. My personal journey required that I look for the answer everywhere else first, before I could appreciate and know the Truth inside me.

Getting rid of the "junk"

In my 40s, I was presented with the idea that I did not have control over my thinking, and it was highly possible my ego had been driving me on autopilot. I was told the way to find out for sure was by doing some simple exercises.

I've always been a student of personal development, but at this point in my life I hadn't experienced a true breakthrough moment, where all the pieces come together and how to make everything work for you finally makes sense. So, I had no expectations with the exercises.

I performed them as suggested and it was impossible to argue with the results. I was shocked at how reactive and negative my thinking was. There was zero doubt that my own thinking, completely created by me had been causing all my pain.

I immediately made the decision to take back control of my thoughts and re-define myself. I cleaned out "the junk" and re-programmed my mind with the Truth by using the simplest tools imaginable.

I was finally able to quiet that little voice inside my head, who was always eager to point out my shortcomings, and I erased the recordings of my failures permanently. This was the ultimate game changer in my life, a true breakthrough.

The change was so dramatic that my family often wondered who this new dad was. Everything good in my life increased, and what I didn't want in my life seemed to vanish into thin air. My health, happiness, relationships, business, and finances all greatly improved.

I have plenty of experience with business, financial, and spiritual trial and error, and I can confidently tell you this: When you follow the steps and exercises in this book, it is impossible not to experience a major improvement in your life.

I know this to be true because I have personally proven it. Everything given to you in this book I have used to bring myself out of emotional and spiritual poverty into a life full of happiness, success, and abundance.

I have written Think A Better Thought™ to help you hack into a new way of thinking, with tools for you to implement immediately, so that you don't have to spend years running around searching for what truly works to have real peace in your life like I did.

YOU MUST TAKE ACTION.

Starting with the next chapter, you will be given a training exercise and an opportunity to go deeper. If you want to experience positive results, practice the exercises. They work, but only if you give them the opportunity to work. There are enough examples for you to find the exercises that work best for you and adapt them to your best method of learning.

A free workbook is available for you to download or use online at Thinkabetterthought.com that includes each Chapter Summary, Training Exercise and Go Deeper opportunity.

Reading the exercises and thinking about them will not work. You can think about what you want to change, but if you do not take action, you will never see those changes come to life. The concepts and tools are easy to use, but simply reading them does nothing. Take action.

Certain ideas, concepts, and exercises are repeated several times, and some chapters are short. This is intentional. Think A Better Thought™ is designed for you to exercise your mind. Repetition is the mother of mastery, and your proficiency increases with each use. The benefits you will receive in this book will be realized by DOING the exercises as soon as you have the initial concept of them and continuing to practice them with everlasting persistence.

Practicing the exercises every day is the action needed to realize what you desire. This book has no hidden secrets. I have not "set up" something for you to figure out. My desire is for you to immediately realize a positive change in your life by putting what I am suggesting into action. ⚲

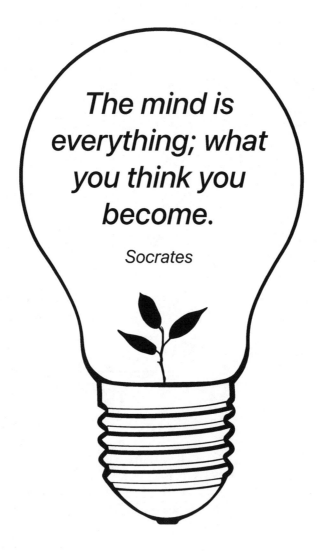

The mind is everything; what you think you become.

Socrates

 # CHAPTER 2
YOUR MIND'S GARDEN

You have the ability to think what you want to think at any moment.

To prove this point, I invite you to Think A Better Thought™ right now.

Take five seconds and improve what you're currently thinking.

If you're thinking about food for instance, turn that thought into one of the most delicious meals you have ever had.

If you're thinking about what a person is or is not doing, turn that thought into how grateful you are to have them in your life.

It truly is that simple to take control of your thought and instantly make it better. You can turn your life into what you really desire by having the will to control your thought.

It requires great discipline to think what you want to think, especially if you've developed the bad habit of thinking negatively like I did.

How much of your will is required to control your thought? One experience most people can relate to is changing their diet or exercise program to lose weight.

If you are used to eating 3,000 calories a day and all of a sudden cut your calorie intake to 2,000 a day, you naturally feel hungry. Your body is not used to receiving less because you have programmed your body for 3,000 calories. Your body creates hunger pains to motivate you to feed it more food.

You have to have the discipline to say no to yourself if you want to see results in weight loss. If you give in and eat more, you risk not losing the desired weight or even worse, you risk potentially gaining weight.

Monitoring your thought and making it the best thought possible is not optional for success, it is an absolute requirement. Conscious, deliberate thinking is the hardest work we do, and you're about to learn a very effective way to do it.

Here's an example of how I used to struggle with my thoughts. This happened nearly every night for years, what seemed like thousands of random thoughts coming out of nowhere and in no particular order.

Here's how it would usually go:

In bed, I would have every intention of quickly falling asleep and then out of nowhere, BAM! A random thought would flash inside my head and then with lightning speed thought after thought after thought.

I could not believe my mind could produce that many different thoughts consecutively. They came so fast that I couldn't even take one and concentrate on it. It was like watching a dog in a park bustling with thousands of squirrels, not knowing which one to chase, frozen in place.

The most troublesome part about this was that the thoughts had zero value to me — all these thoughts were of past disappointments or worry about future events.

Over time I found that I was not alone, and that many of my peers had the same experience of not being able to fall asleep or waking up with the same thoughts of past disappointments and worries about future events.

We shared our miseries about lack of sleep, which seemed normal, a part of our everyday life. I would look at my wife and wonder why it was so easy for her to just fall asleep. I was even jealous of the dog and his ability to instantly drift off.

I had no idea how far off I was. I had accepted that not being able to fall asleep quickly at night, with thousands of random thoughts running through my head was a normal side effect of being a business owner.

The truth is that my mind needed a massive weeding out.

The garden and your mind.

Several times in this book I compare planting a seed in soil to you planting a thought in your mind. I repeat it because I want you to get it. This is the illustration that finally made it clear to me how I was preventing good things from happening in my life.

Pretend that you desire to plant a beautiful rose garden with many rose bushes. You plan out exactly where you want each bush, thinking about how beautiful your garden will look when all the roses are blooming.

You plant and carefully watch over your rose bushes, providing just the right amount of fertilizer and water. Soon, you start to notice rose buds and those buds eventually bloom into beautiful roses. Each year as you continue to care for your rose bushes, they grow and flourish, becoming even more beautiful than you had imagined when you made the decision to have a rose garden.

Now let's compare this rose garden to the garden in your mind. The rose garden is like an idea you have. This idea or thought coming from your conscious mind (the finished beautiful rose garden) is planted in your subconscious mind (the soil). The soil and plants work together with minimal help from you (watering and fertilizing) to make the rose bushes grow, bud, and bloom.

Your thoughts planted into your subconscious mind produce the effects (the rose garden) of your thought. When you correctly nurture your thoughts, the effects of your thoughts, your ideas, grow into what you desire.

Now imagine that just as soon as your rose bushes start to bud, you spray weed killer on them. The buds quickly dry up and your rose garden dies.

You wouldn't plant a rose bush and then poison it, but this is exactly what most people do with their ideas without even realizing it. The problem is that we are not taught the right way to nurture our thoughts so that they can grow into the finished ideas. Instead, most people are programmed with negative, poisonous thinking. Just think for a moment about what you are exposed to every day.

The news media is always selling you the worst possible scenario, telling stories of war, death, disease, and conflict. Social media channels are full of stories of envy, pride, loss, fear, and deception. Everywhere you go you see advertisements for products to fix problems in your life you didn't even know you had.

You cannot control what the world around you is doing or thinking, but you can learn to break the habit of being programmed by outside influences. You can also learn how to clear out the weeds and dead growth in your mind that have prevented you from blossoming.

These weeds are lack of persistence, fear, resentment, condemnation, worry, negativity, pain, and belief in failure. They must be cleared out and kept out for you to see your ideas realized.

Negative thinking is the equivalent of spraying weed poison on your ideas and dreams.

Nothing can happen in your life without thought first, whether it is subconscious thought like the beating of your heart or conscious thought like choosing to open a door.

We are constantly planting new thoughts into our minds. It is your choice as to what seeds of thought you plant, your ideas. It is your choice to nurture and allow them to mature, or to poison and destroy them by allowing negative thinking in.

The Truth is nothing happens without thought first, and YOU are 100% responsible for all your thoughts.

Ask yourself if you have ever done anything or had anything done to you that originated without a thought. Thought always is the first cause. Knowing this truth, how beneficial is it to Think A Better Thought™ as often as you can?

Taking back control of my thought is one of the greatest gifts I have ever received, so incredible that it has driven me to share my personal experience with you.

How did I take back control of my thinking?

The short answer is that I stopped judging myself and instead, really took the position of, "Let's just observe and not judge what I'm thinking any more. All truths withstand all observation. All falsehoods simply vanish when they are observed for what they are."

When I was able to make a pact with myself that if I observe this and it's not true, it's okay to dump it; if it is true, it's okay to keep it...that's when things really started to shift.

I began to see that my best thinking continually unfolded in the present moment. I learned I could approach myself with compassion instead of judgment. I could take responsibility every step of the way for everything I'd done or everything that had happened to me.

Employing true observation and real acceptance caused the turning point in my life.

CHAPTER SUMMARY

Judging people, places, and things completely prevented me from enjoying life.

I was frequently offended by the thinking or ideas of others. I engaged in arguments. I would get upset with news stories, social media posts, and entities with no personal connection.

Even though I'd heard other people say that you have to put down the judge's gavel, I didn't truly get it until I had experienced enough pain. I thought I was supposed put the judge's gavel down when looking at others. I broke out of my prison when I completely stopped judging myself.

The day I stopped judging myself is the day I really started to get into spiritual shape.

True success in my personal and professional life came when I really stopped judging my thinking. When I completely let go of what I thought was my duty to judge, it felt like taking the weight of the world off my shoulders.

TRAINING EXERCISE

Ask yourself, "How often am I judging others or myself?"

Then ask, "Does judging others or myself have any benefit for me?"

Don't do anything more than asking the questions and observing your answers. We're simply starting by learning to shine the light of observation on your thoughts.

GO DEEPER

Do you ever feel exhausted from your thoughts?

It makes sense, because we have about 80,000 thoughts per day and if we're not careful, then they're like mosquitoes that keep buzzing in our ears. You're trying to swat them away, but they keep biting you, and you're just losing yourself in the madness.

First, I had to learn when I did not have conscious control of my thought. Using these steps exposed how my ego would take control over my thinking. Performing these exercises regularly will train your brain to recognize and prevent attempts by your ego to regain control of your thinking.

Step 1 - Think of a past experience in your life, one that was extremely pleasurable; one of the best moments of your life. Write your memory down on the line below. It can be a simple description. You know the memory.

_____

Step 2 - It is best for this step that you have a quiet place you can sit or lie down and relax.

Take your memory above and focus only on that one, positive thought for 20 seconds. Really try and go back to that memory and feel how good you felt...really feel it. Time yourself and see if you can focus your thought on that one memory for a full 20 seconds without any other thought. Do this now.

How did you do? If you did not get the full 20 seconds in, do not be troubled. Persist. Keep working at it. The human mind can be distracted every six seconds. If this exercise is new to you, it is not fair for you to expect to get it right the first time. Don't give up. Use persistence to learn how to have a full 20 seconds of uninterrupted, positive thought.

The first time I did this exercise, I focused on a memory of our family's vacation to Iceland. I was able to stay focused on this memory for only three seconds before I started thinking about something else. Not being able to focus on a single, positive thought for 20 straight seconds was a clear demonstration of my ego's attempt and ability to take control of my thinking.

Take control back. Focus on your memory again for 20 seconds. Do this until you can focus exclusively on that memory for 20 seconds straight without interruption. If you must, demand from yourself that you do this. If it takes you a full hour or day to accomplish this, persist to do it. This is a critical skill in regaining control of your thought.

Are you ready to see how determined and crazy your ego can be?

Step 3 – Take your memory and expand to the entire experience. Re-live it if you can for 20 minutes or longer. You can also take other positive experiences and add them in if you would like. Try to hold consistent, positive thought in your mind for 20 minutes straight.

23

If you are not able to do this for 20 minutes, persist until you do. It is important to remember that you are not competing against anyone. The truth is that you are now recognizing a big roadblock that has been standing between you and your success, your ego. Beating yourself up has zero benefit to you. Observing has 100 % benefit. ⚲

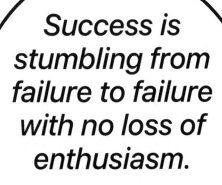

Success is stumbling from failure to failure with no loss of enthusiasm.

Winston Churchill

 # CHAPTER 3

PERSISTENCE IS THE LIFEBLOOD OF SUCCESS

I thought I was successful and bullet proof at 24.

I had a nearly perfect credit score, I was newly married, we had our first son, and had just moved to Midland, Texas. That was March 1st, 1996. By July 4th of that same year, I was living in poverty on a combined income of $1,000 a month with no credit or credibility.

Collection calls came all day and night. I hated the phone. I hated the mail. Everyone wanted something from me that I could not give them, money.

I looked at myself as a total failure.

I was in a deep hole of debt and depression. The hole was dirty and muddy with sharp rocks and sticks. It was painful, and it took years to climb out. I could have let go of the little progress I made climbing out of it at any time and fallen back in.

Staying down was easy and required zero effort. I had no idea how I was going to get out of that situation. The only thing I was able to do was decide that no matter what it took I was going to get out.

There were two things that helped my climb out of that hole: the first was making the decision to get out. The second was persistence, backed by the unconditional love and support of my wife, Dedee. She never stopped believing in me and pushed me to be better every step of the way.

I read books, went to conferences, and practiced what I was learning over and over. I tried every technique, and while I still experienced plenty of setbacks, I also started to move forward, one step at a time.

Over 20 years later my wife and I own a successful business with multiple locations. We have a blessed life today, because of the Law of Persistence.

The one thing I can say contributed most to my success is that I didn't give up, and that my wife never gave up on me.

There is only one thing I believe you have to be perfect at, and that one thing is Persistence.

Don't quit.

Don't give in.

Never give up.

Keep moving forward.

If you fail, don't be afraid to fail again.

You can never succeed if you give up. This is an absolute guarantee.

It's truly the lack of persistence that kills off more dreams than anything else.

Great stories aren't made up of easy climbs to the top of the mountain — they're made up of major trials and tribulations. They're often of common people who started with nothing, yet the one key to their great triumph was their persistence.

If they had quit, there would have been no story. What if Thomas Edison had quit after light bulb failure No. 8,573?

Persistence is the lifeblood of success. You can write your "Greatest Story Ever", but only if you do not quit.

You can re-gain control of your thoughts, but without constant practice of the tools given you will lose the ability to think what you want to think.

Napoleon Hill, author of *Think and Grow Rich*, studied Thomas Edison and Henry Ford for nearly 25 years, and attributed one, single trait to their tremendous success and achievement, ***persistence.***

If you had asked me what I thought was the greatest factor of their success before reading Napoleon Hill's writing, I would have told you "they were obviously geniuses, smarter than the average person." But not according to Hill. Persistence was the "one thing" both Edison and Ford had in common. Over 100 years later both of their ideas live on in abundance.

Persistence will be your best friend, helping you master and keep control of your thoughts. When you make mistakes and experience failures, you can rely on persistence to get you back on track and sharpen the focus on your ideas.

Our culture has become accustomed to immediate gratification. The age of internet shopping and same day delivery, many times within the hour, have programmed us with unrealistic expectations for success. We want and expect everything now.

While so many of us want to achieve everything we've ever wanted instantaneously, it's unlikely to happen and in fact, wouldn't benefit us in the ways that we think.

People, places, and things are outside of your control. They can come unannounced into your life at any time. Your work may be criticized by someone. You may have a close relative who needs financial help, depleting your savings. There may be a natural disaster that destroys your home. You could lose your job.

There are countless things out there that can knock you off course. Few, if any, great business leaders would tell you they had an easy road to success. Instead, they would tell you about unexpected challenges and roadblocks that had to be managed and overcome. If you asked them to give you one piece of advice, most, if not all, would tell you this, "Don't quit."

It is easy to believe that if you are not successful right away, you never will be. It is easy to accept the criticism of others. It is easy to think something is too hard to do. When we believe these thoughts, we are poisoning our garden, and we quit.

This is the one thing we can never do. We can never quit. You are going to make mistakes, be criticized, and have challenges. You are going to "accidentally" poison your garden. Humans are not perfect, and life is not fair.

Change is constant and unavoidable. You must persist through change, failure, events, people, places, circumstances, and things out of your control.

If you fail, observe why, learn from it, and don't make the same mistake again. You may make a different mistake that causes a similar failure. If this happens, accept it, learn from it, and move on. Your will to never quit makes all the difference in overcoming failure and turning it into success.

Success follows the Law of Nature.

Nature gives us great examples of how to work and evolve. Take the oak tree, for example.

The oak tree starts out as a simple acorn and does not mature enough to produce new acorns usually until it is 50 years old, but once it does, the oak can produce acorns for the next 700-1,000 years. One oak tree can produce approximately 10 million acorns during its lifespan.

The oak tree's growth is slow and steady, always advancing. Do you expect the oak to immediately mature after the acorn is planted? You can have this expectation, but the reality is that the tiny acorn must follow the Law of Nature to grow into a mighty, giant oak.

Ten million acorns created by the planting of one is a significant return on investment, but it does not happen overnight.

It's easy to think about an acorn being planted and maturing naturally into an oak tree. If you met someone who expected to plant an acorn and realize a fully-grown tree within a few weeks, you would not put any faith behind their expectation because you know the Law of Nature does not allow this to happen.

Planting the acorn and continuing to support growth by watering, all the while knowing in your mind that one day, a full-grown oak will be standing before you is the demonstration of perfect faith and belief in the idea of the oak tree.

Why is it so hard then for us to believe our ideas are maturing naturally as well? How do we think wrong? We lose faith in our ideas by not believing that one day, our idea will be standing before us, fully matured.

We do this by choosing to look at our lives from the perspective of what we don't have, keeping us stuck in the same place. You must have right thinking to keep your attention focused in the present on your ideas and dreams.

Right thinking is simple but not easy. Right thinking requires faithful persistence. But what is faithful persistence?

Believing your idea is already a reality. This is faithful persistence. Let's go back to the rose garden and oak to illustrate.

Your faith is unbroken, knowing the rose garden and oak will grow and produce when you planted them. Your rose garden, beautiful with roses is the reality you saw when you planted the rose bushes and as you continued to water them. The mighty oak producing millions of acorns is the reality you saw when the acorn was pushed into the soil.

What the seeds, roots, and soil did together was out of your control. Your control was the first cause, the thought, the idea of experiencing a fully matured rose garden and oak tree. Your control was:

> The action required, planting.
>
> Persistence, watering with faith, knowing the rose garden and oak would mature.

The idea I am illustrating with this example is that no matter what happens with your plans, hold the end result as achieved with unbreakable, persistent faith.

When something doesn't work, you simply haven't discovered the right or best way to make it work. If you are locked in on only one way to do something and it doesn't work, you're left with no options.

Your job is to create the idea (planting the seed) and persistently hold with faith your idea is a reality (watering), just like the matured oak and roses. How your idea evolves, grows, and matures is not up to you. This is where most people get permanently thrown off course.

They are so stubborn about their dreams happening a certain way that they only place their focus on their plans being carried out that same way, and they lose their focus on the big picture, the end result.

They are more worried about what the seed and soil are doing together than experiencing the matured growth. When their plans don't work, they see a failed idea and quit.

Plans are definitely needed to carry out any idea, but you need to keep your focus and faith on the end result. This focus will deliver your plans to you. Your plans could be perfect, or they may need to be changed. You may need an entire set of new plans, but if you do not persist with keeping your focus and faith on the end result, you will never realize it.

Winston Churchill illustrated faithful persistence perfectly when he said, "Success is stumbling from failure to failure with no loss of enthusiasm." Persistence is something you do. You don't have to learn it, you just start doing it, and the more you do it, the more persistence you will have.

CHAPTER SUMMARY

Taking back control of your mind is not hard. Staying in control of your thinking is the real work.

I know that persistence is the foundational ingredient of my success. I like to think of the practice of persistence as daily nourishment and training.

What would happen if you were not persistent about eating? You would suffer the effects of not nourishing your body. You would become weak and eventually die.

Nourish yourself daily by being persistent in monitoring your thoughts. Train yourself daily with the exercises presented. Be persistent. You'll be amazed at the results if you simply persist.

One of the best uses of your time would be to persistently eliminate the word "try" from your vocabulary. The way to get more persistence is to start persisting more. You cannot try to be persistent. You can only be persistent.

Trying and failure go hand-in-hand and never equate to doing. Quitting only guarantees one thing, failure. If you want to really do something, then do it, continue to do it, and do not stop doing it.

TRAINING EXERCISE

We are going to start with something easy, the word "try."

Monitor your words and thoughts today.

Keep count of how many times you say or think about "trying" to do something versus actually "doing" that thing.

First, you need to understand how often you may be thinking limited thoughts. Soon, you'll learn how to recognize, remove, and replace them with unlimited thoughts.

GO DEEPER

What do you think of when you read the word "mastery?"

Do you want to be a master of success?

How do you become a master of any one thing?

A person becomes a master by repeating the basic exercises of that one thing over and over and over again. They do not try to master more than one thing at a time. They focus only on one. A master does not practice thousands of different exercises a few times each to learn their skill.

Masters practice the same few exercises thousands and thousands of times. The results of their practice may not look fruitful in the beginning, but over time by doing the same drills and exercises over and over, they become better and better. Their skill level increases and accelerates with every move, and with persistent, daily work they eventually become a master.

Years ago, NASA conducted an experiment to determine what kind of effect being in a weightless environment for long periods of time would have on astronauts. NASA fitted the astronaut candidates with goggles that completely flipped their vision 180 degrees. The candidates wore the goggles 24/7.

An amazing event happened on the 26th day. One of the astronaut's brains completely flipped the image back to what it would be without the goggles. Even though he was still wearing the goggles all the time, everything now looked normal. Within the next several days the same thing happened to all of the other astronaut candidates.

NASA continued the experiment with new astronaut candidates and created a variable, allowing the goggles to come off for short periods of time. The candidates would still wear the goggles for 30 or more total days, but interrupted with short periods where the goggles would be removed.

The neural adaptation never occurred with this variable. The astronauts' vision remained unchanged, even when a total of 30 days of wearing the goggles was achieved. It always took 25-30 consecutive days of constant, 24/7 wearing of the goggles for the brain to accept it as normal.

What does this experiment tell us? It takes 25-30 days of consistent action to create a change in our neural adaptation. If you want to change, you must be persistent and never give up! ☒

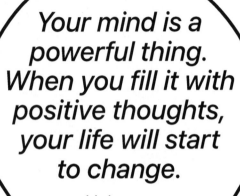

Your mind is a powerful thing. When you fill it with positive thoughts, your life will start to change.

Unknown

CHAPTER 4

WHO IS "THAT LITTLE VOICE INSIDE YOUR HEAD?"

Have you ever had an experience where you asked yourself, "Where in the heck did that thought come from?"

I've had thousands of these experiences, and most of the time my thought was fear based, focused on the worst possible outcome. I developed an automatic "but what if" negative response for nearly everything.

My first reaction to any idea or suggestion by someone else became, "No, I don't think that would work. I don't think I would enjoy that."

On the flip side, whenever I had an idea or suggestion that was not immediately accepted, I would say or think, "I'm right and you're wrong. You need to follow what I'm saying."

This "say no first, I'm always right" mentality became so bad that my wife had to preface anything she wanted to do by first saying, "I need you to come from a place of yes."

I might not have verbally said, "No," right away, but the thought of "No!" inside my head was automatic.

I did not know I had a problem with reacting to life. I had the belief that this automatic "no" was intelligence and experience at work. The truth is that I had allowed myself to be unconsciously programmed by an internal voice I did not know.

Ask yourself, "What am I thinking right now?"

Then ask yourself, "Is this thought hurting me, or is this thought helping me?" You could also ask yourself, "Does this thought have any benefit for me?"

Our thoughts are either helping us or not. Simple enough, right?

Now, pause for just a second and ask yourself this question: "Who is thinking this?"

Discovering the true identity revealed by asking, "Who is thinking this?" was my breakthrough moment. This discovery...it was the "one thing" that brought all the lessons together, clearly identifying the roadblock that had been standing in the way of what I truly desired to experience in my life, my ego.

The roadblock had been hiding in plain sight. It was that little voice living inside my head, the voice who has full access to all my memories, bringing them up with perfect timing.

This voice is given all kinds of names like ego, paradigms, negative thinking, etc. You can name it however you desire, but for the purposes of this book I will use the name, ego.

I like to think of our relationship with our ego as similar to the popular skit between Lucy and Charlie Brown. Charlie Brown represents you. Lucy is your ego. Every time you run up to kick the football, she pulls it away, so that you fall flat on your back, thinking, "Good grief!"

Even when you think you have her outsmarted or you trust that this time, she's not going to pull the ball back...she still does with perfect timing, always landing you flat on your back!

In my experience, the ego is wily, mischievous, and operates from a place of protection.

I have participated in several seasons of play in the "ego laboratory", and I've come to know that my ego bases everything on past experiences I've had, re-living memories to keep me in a place of fear that prevents me from moving forward and getting what I want out of life.

Many of us might know the ego as that thing that's fueled us for many years — at least it was for me. I worked for the accolades and awards.

38

I worked for the money and material things. I was not humble and didn't know the definition of humility. Instead, I figured I could muscle my way through everything.

When I was in my early 20s, I had the opportunity to sell life insurance and mutual funds while still in college. I got my licenses from the State of Texas and the Federal Securities and Exchange Commission, full of confidence that a high-paying career in financial services was right around the corner. People in my company were earning six figures left and right, so I was certain easy money was in sight!

Except...as a 23-year-old salesman for financial services, I had little credibility when consulting families about their financial futures.

I struggled to make sales. And, the ones I did make? Well, they were to family members who bought purely out of pity. I finally gave up after two years of pure defeat and looked for another job.

When I started a new job at a television station, I flat out lied about my previous financial services gig in Houston, boldly claiming that I earned six-figures multiple times over.

If I had done that well before, what the heck was I doing with a job in advertising sales at this TV station for $30,000 a year? I maintained the lie, knowing full well that my colleagues knew I was a joke.

My ego won, but I lost in every other respect.

I didn't learn any skills or tools that could've propelled my success forward. Instead, stuck in my lies, I stayed small and kept the fear of failure chained to me incredibly tight.

That "fear of failure" we often have is our ego using past experiences against our designs for future growth. That little voice inside our heads telling us we aren't good enough or we don't have enough experience is our ego talking. This is crazy thinking with no value or benefit to us, ever.

What is really crazy is how often we have crazy thinking. We keep ourselves stuck in a rut, wondering why the same things keep happening over and over. We must make the effort to take full thought control instead of letting our ego driven thoughts manage our past, present, and future.

This requires constant monitoring of our thoughts, and a forgiving attitude when we get off course.

Our egos have a very clever way of tripping us up with perfect timing.

Have you ever had an experience where you were "almost there" and then were tripped up right before change was coming into your life? Well, your ego knows you better than anyone else.

Your ego knows everything about you. It possesses an entire history of your life. It knows all your secrets. It knows all your thoughts. Your ego has all this available and ready to use against you at any time.

Your ego doesn't like change.

Change isn't safe to your ego, and it uses everything available to prevent change. The truth is that your ego only has the past to work with. You aren't living in the past. You are living now.

Your ego can actually be used beneficially, because it constantly points out all the different false beliefs you have allowed yourself to purchase and store away over the years.

If you are paying attention and really want to clear them out, start asking, "What am I thinking right now? Is it hurting me or helping me?"

Do not judge what you are thinking. Just observe your thoughts.

Ask yourself if you created this thought or if your ego did. Again, do not judge what you are thinking. Just observe the thought.

If it is from your ego, then ask why and how the thought got there. Observe the answer, don't judge it. The more you do this the more you will start to see what thoughts are coming from you and which ones are coming from your ego.

The reason why I say "observe" the answer and do not "judge" the answer is this: ***All truth withstands observation***. If something is really true, and you honestly observe or question that truth, you will be able to determine it to be true, even if it takes some time.

Judgment, however, creates an immediate belief.

But surely, it is right to judge, yes? There are obvious things in life that are easy to judge as true or not, like whether a dinner plate is hot or cold. I'm sure you are thinking this, and it is true. But what you have to be careful with is creating the habit of judgment.

Your ego judges and creates beliefs, both true and false. When you are constantly judging what you are thinking, like I did for most of my life, there is always the risk of making the wrong judgment, but even worse...you are more likely to be unconsciously giving control of your thoughts and life to your ego, thinking negative and limiting thoughts.

> What am I thinking?

> Does this thought have any benefit for me?

> Who is thinking this?

> Why am I thinking this?

These questions are all to help you learn the difference between unconscious thoughts from your ego, and conscious thoughts of success, the real seeds you want to plant into your subconscious mind.

Your job is to be persistent in asking yourself these questions so you can be certain that you are in control of what seeds are planted in the garden of your mind.

CHAPTER SUMMARY

Which voice do we need to zero in on?

The one who says, "No, you can't do that."

This is the voice who speaks with doubt when you're working to make positive changes in your life. This is the voice trying to defeat your persistence telling you it's ok to give up. This is the voice who keeps you stuck in the same place. You hear this voice when you set any goal, and then immediately doubt your ability to achieve it.

Unfortunately, society, culture, and family have often taught us to think this way.

In fact, one of the first words a child learns is the word, "no."

We are consumed with incoming messages and images, both solicited and not, especially if we spend hours in front of televisions, computers and smart phones. It's easy to become hypnotized and tune out, which is when our egos take control of our consciousness.

This negative voice inside our heads is the enemy within you, your ego.

Our ego works against us to prevent change. The only thing our egos have to use against us to prevent change is the past. This is important, and worth taking a few moments to let sink in.

Everything our egos use against us is based on past experiences.

Buying what our egos are selling us is absolutely crazy thinking because we are never living in the past. We are always here in the present.

Is there any benefit to beating ourselves up over past experiences? We can't change the past. The past has already happened. Re-living the past keeps us stuck, doubting with fear, and unable to realize what we desire.

TRAINING EXERCISE

That little voice inside your head is telling you you're not good enough. It's telling you you're stuck in a rut. It's keeping you from breaking free.

Your ego can be especially effective in tripping you up, just the way that Lucy does to Charlie Brown.

Have you ever felt like you got "tripped up" right before a positive change was coming into your life?

When you're successful and you prove your old beliefs wrong, your ego can feel like a madman on the loose inside your head.

The problem is, your ego knows you better than anyone else, so it's got all the tools to use against you to keep itself safe by keeping you small.

Thankfully, you're not living in the past. You're living in the NOW.

It's time to explore what your ego is having you believe, so you can choose a better, newer thought.

Ask yourself, "What am I thinking right now?"

Follow that with the next question, "Is this thought helping or hurting me?"

We're not going to judge any of your responses here.

We're just using the powers of observation to help you gain clarity on what you're thinking. The more you see where your negative thoughts are coming from, the more you will be able to choose a better next thought.

GO DEEPER

It is important to make sure we have a clear definition of our ego and its purpose moving forward. Ego is defined as "a person's sense of self-esteem or self-importance, the part of the mind that mediates between the conscious and the unconscious and is responsible for reality testing and a sense of personal identity, a conscious thinking subject." This definition is from dictionary.com. This definition gives the impression that the ego is useful. Surely, it is important to have a sense of self-esteem and importance, a personal identity.

What is not included in the definition are the words "positive" and "negative." Is it more important to have a positive self-esteem than a negative one? What about our personal identity? How important is it to live with a positive personal identity versus a negative one?

Why are we not taught about our egos in school or even church? It makes perfect sense to learn that our egos are conscious thinking subjects responsible for reality testing in our lives and for our personal identity. If our egos are consciously thinking subjects, then where are we when our egos are conscious? Unconscious? I could have saved myself a lot of time and heartache if I had learned early in life what I know today about my ego.

The ego operates in a state of protection. It does not want to experience pain or misfortune. A state of protection is achieved by having no change in your life. If nothing changes, then nothing changes. That is the rationale of the ego.

Change could bring pain, failure or embarrassment. The ego has no desire to experience these things. The ego's desire is to be exalted, self-justified, in control. You can never rid yourself of your ego, but you can learn to recognize its Jekyll and Hyde thinking. You can gain full control over it. You can learn to silence it without offending. You can learn to live with your ego and use it to be totally beneficial.

44

What is really important is not beating yourself up when you give your ego control. It is going to happen. Your ego will always be with you and when given the opportunity, your ego will engage. Now that we have exposed our egos, we need to move straight to taking control back from them and using them to enhance, not damage our lives. ⅄

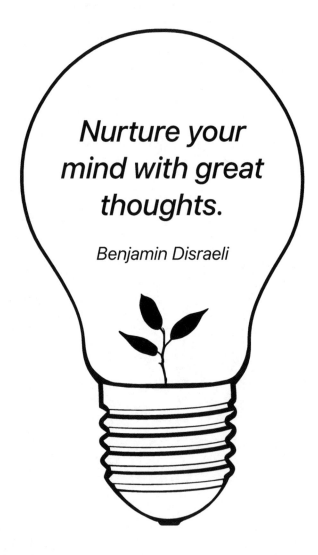

Nurture your
mind with great
thoughts.

Benjamin Disraeli

CHAPTER 5
WHY YOU NEED TO SWEAT IT OUT

If you are worried or anxious, then you are either living in the past or the future, and your ego is selling you on why you need to retreat and play it safe. If you are feeling normal, good, or even happy, then you are present, have control, and are thinking positively.

You've just been made aware of an exceptional tool for monitoring your thoughts, clearly defining negative and positive ones.

This tool is your feelings.

If you are feeling good, then everything is right with your thought and you are positive. Stay there, feeling good. If you are not feeling good, your thoughts are negative. When this happens, simply ask yourself why you are feeling that way. What thought is behind that feeling? Is it true? Remember not to judge or beat yourself up when this happens. The magic happens exclusively through observation.

Observe what and why you are thinking the way you are. The more you observe without any judgment the more control you gain.

Here's the thing: we all have a past. Every single one of us. Even the ones who look like they have it together on social media — we all have "something", and our egos know every last detail. Our egos have even been nice enough to dramatize many of those "somethings."

This is why it's vital to start by sweating it out. Sweat out the crap. Get rid of the shame. Give yourself a fair chance at winning by letting go of everything that's holding you back.

I was born in Albuquerque, New Mexico. My mother taught school while my father was finishing his degree at the University of New Mexico. We were very poor, but I did not know the difference between being poor and being wealthy at that age.

One day, I remember my mom was cooking at the stove and my father was standing behind her, screaming at her while she cooked. I saw her becoming increasingly upset, so I purposefully fell backwards and started crying. It worked. My father left her to come pick me up.

This is the only memory I have of my parents' marriage.

When I was two, my parents divorced, and I moved with my mother from Albuquerque to Wheeler, Texas. Left alone with my very protective mother who had fresh wounds from a broken marriage, I was raised in a deeply fear-based environment.

She would often use the worst-case scenario to motivate me to be "safe," even saying things like, "You can't go to the restaurant bathroom by yourself, because you might get your balls cut off." This scared the hell out of me as a kid, but I place no blame on her for doing this. She had lost her marriage, and there was no way in hell she planned on losing her child too. She was doing everything she knew how at that time to protect me in the best way.

I learned to look at everything first with, "What's the worst thing that can happen?" Instead of "What is the best possible outcome?"

When you look for what could always go wrong guess what happens? Things go wrong because "going wrong" is where you're focusing your thoughts. You're planting seeds of "going wrong." Shifting the focus of your thoughts from "going wrong" to "going right" is a move that will benefit you every time without fail.

So...let's take a moment and reflect upon the thoughts that you're having...

Do you find that your thoughts are repetitive?

Are they the same thoughts you've had the day before?

Do you often feel stuck, yet can't figure out why?

Are you feeling like you're re-living the same moments, events, and problems over and over again?

Do you wish you could simply turn off your mind and find some peace already?

Living with a fear-based mentality at such an impressionable age, I know firsthand what's required to shift your perspective into one that actually serves you.

I've come to believe that success is completely dependent upon a solid foundation of persistence in right thinking.

Understanding our beginnings helps us understand how our minds work. We start to know what our triggers are and how to figure out ways to both heal them or bend them to our advantage. By focusing on the beginning here now, we'll be able to accelerate the results you want to see.

CHAPTER SUMMARY

It is easy to point the finger at someone else for your problems, especially when you truly have been wronged. We all have our "junk." Whether someone gave it to us, or we made it on our own, having some "junk" at some point in our lives is part of being human. Where we get tripped up is that most of us think that our "junk" is worse than everyone else's.

You can find fault in your boss for being stuck in your career. You can get upset about politics and paying taxes. It doesn't take much effort to place blame outside of yourself for anything.

Ask yourself if blaming other people has any benefit for you.

TRAINING EXERCISE

Honor the people in your past and present where they're honorable.

In order to set the right foundation for your mindset moving forward, it's imperative that you take a good hard look at what got you to where you are now.

Usually, there's someone that we have to forgive, and a thought we have to get rid of, because it's as though our minds are infected.

For today, your training day exercise is to acknowledge that you have an infected way of thinking and to commit to cleaning it out.

It's time to match up with your ego.

Ask yourself:

> What am I thinking right now?
> Is this helping or hurting me?
> Why am I thinking this?
> Is this happening now?
> Is this thought real?

Use the powers of observation to help you gain clarity on what you're thinking. Do not worry or try to change your thoughts, simply observe them.

Remember the magic happens exclusively through observation.

GO DEEPER

So many of us have negative thoughts without realizing it and we create these thoughts because this pattern of questioning our worthiness or of what's not possible is stuck on auto-pilot. How often have you thought about something you desire, yet the very next second, you tell yourself you can't have it?

Doing this to ourselves is similar to planting a beautiful garden full of roses, watering and nurturing the flowers, and just when they're ready to be picked, poisoning them instead.

Stop neutralizing your desires or doubting that you can have them and start by taking all that crap from your past and turning it into manure that can fertilize your dreams.

Think A Better Thought™ than you currently are now. Focus only on that thought for twenty seconds or longer.

Go even deeper by thinking of one of the most positive experiences of your life. Take that experience and focus your thought on it for twenty minutes or longer. Use this experience as your "go to life preserver" when your ego starts to create doubt.⍍

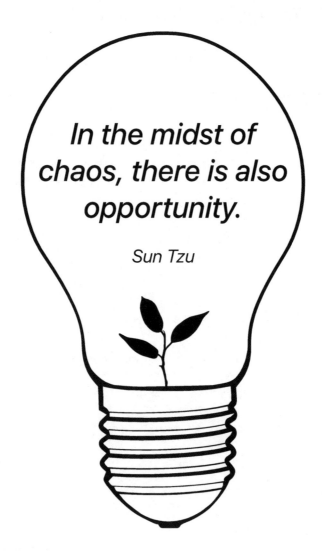

In the midst of chaos, there is also opportunity.

Sun Tzu

CHAPTER 6
WHAT YOU HAVE TO LOOK OUT FOR

A real understanding of the negative power of your ego and most importantly, the ability to recognize when your ego is on the attack and stop the attack is a skill you must master.

Why? Because you will never be able to eliminate your ego. Your ego is always going to be with you, but you can learn how to work with it. You can learn to limit your ego's influence over your conscious thinking so that you can keep your focus on the good of what you are desiring.

I look at matching up with my ego like playing a game. In the team sports that I played, there was a basic process used to plan a win:

1. Scout the opponent.
2. Identify their top players.
3. Identify their weaker players.
4. Find what our best match-ups were, as in where our strengths exposed their weaknesses.
5. Attack the other team's weaknesses.
6. Stick with the game plan.

Just like in the book, *The Art of War,* you don't attack strengths — you attack weaknesses. We don't want to match strengths with strengths with our egos because that'd be like playing tic-tac-toe, where no one's going to win. We actually have a better chance of losing because while we may let our conscious guard down...our ego never will.

You have probably asked yourself enough questions by this point to see that your ego attacks when your defenses are down.

My ego knows every secret I have. When I first learned to take control away from my ego, I was amazed at how easy it was. I was so excited to have learned a skill that was so beneficial to me.

Each day I started and ended with full control of my thought. All I needed to do was think positive thoughts in place of negative thoughts. I did this by asking the simple questions I gave you in Chapter 4.

I had been using this newly learned skill for about two weeks very successfully, and then things went sideways.

I got comfortable, letting my guard down, and one day out of nowhere I was attacked with negative thoughts. I spent a full weekend immersed in stinkin' thinkin'. Everything irritated me. I was miserable.

What made it worse for me is that I knew I had just experienced two of the best "thinking" weeks of my life. I had been free, and now I wasn't.

"What has gone wrong?" I asked myself. I started to judge myself. I became furious with myself. I could not believe I had allowed myself to fall back into negative thinking. It took me two full days to regain control of my thought, and I felt the event had set my progress in reverse.

This was not the only time I allowed my ego to regain control from me. About the same amount of time, two weeks, passed when I experienced another ego attack. The outcome was nearly identical. I questioned whether or not I was capable of staying positive. I feared I would not be able to fully regain control.

I needed help with recognizing a negative thought pattern early.

I asked my wife to call me out for negative thinking the next time she noticed it. I explained why I needed her to do this, that I needed to learn the skill of recognizing a negative thought pattern early, so I could learn the skill of neutralizing it immediately.

Her response was reluctant.

She had experienced over 20 years of my ego already. Being a willing participant in battling it was not a lucrative proposition for her. In her eyes, it only meant potential pain from my ego lashing out at her.

This made me want to conquer my ego even more. I was tired of being irritable, restless, and discontent...even if it was only every two weeks now. I made the decision to eliminate those states from my consciousness.

The first time my wife called me out really irritated me.

How could she say I was being negative? Did she not realize how much time I was spending on positive thinking?

Those thoughts were my ego talking. This time it only took me a day to catch my ego running the show. I was making progress.

The negative thinking time was now down to just one day instead of two. With my wife's help, I had shortened the recovery time.

Today, I can snap out of negative thinking within minutes. Often, I see it coming and stop it before it happens, but sometimes my ego still gets the best of me.

Your ego will still get the best of you too at times, but the more you work at developing the skills to realize when this happens, the quicker you will be able to re-set and get back on track.

Here's another simple tool you can use to regain control.

Throughout your day when you notice feelings, thoughts or actions you desire to eliminate, say this simple word, "Change." Even if you realize hours later that you had a negative thought, say, "Change." This is all you have to do.

You may need to say change many times for the same thought. One I struggle with is irritating drivers. I have easily let aggressive driving get me in a bad mood many times. When I am in a bad mood, I'm not feeling good, and I know my ego is in control.

Today, when I get cut off in traffic and I think about honking my horn or yelling, I say, "Change." Sometimes I have to say, "Change, change, change!"

You may find something that works better for you and that is great. The point is to find a quick and easy tool to help you reset and keep control of your thought when you need it.

CHAPTER SUMMARY

Learning to consciously battle your ego can be like learning a new game or sport to play.

I "practiced" staying in control of my thoughts for two weeks. The practice was in a controlled environment, designed for success. My skills and confidence grew over those two weeks. I felt unbeatable.

But then came game day.

Game day is when your ego attacks your thinking.

There is a good chance that your ego will give you a good 'ol fashioned butt kicking, even after you've been showing up for practice every day for weeks.

You might want to quit, but don't. Instead, practice harder. Controlling your ego is a choice. Choose to take back control of your conscious thinking. You may lose again in a few weeks or even the next day, but it won't be the same kind of butt kicking. In fact, you may even lose to your ego several times, but each time it's by less and less, and you learn new skills along the way.

I used to let my ego pick when game day was. Today I have set the permanent game schedule, and it is always game time. I have learned I am playing the game of life. The game never ends, and the ego is always ready to attack so I stay on guard. I recognize a bad thought by the feeling I get from it. You can do the same.

TRAINING EXERCISE

It's time to clean out your closet.

Make a list of all the things you're DONE with in your life:

Thoughts
Habits
Behaviors
Relationships
Beliefs

Ask yourself if it is healthy and loving for you to keep these things in your life, and as you go through your list say, "Change," out loud for each thing you want to clear out for good. See yourself experiencing the opposite of what you don't want.

GO DEEPER

When you get that queasy feeling in your stomach from fear or you get that headache from anger, this is the moment you need to counter attack with positive thinking.

The physical feelings you have may be different from mine, but you were given these feelings for a reason, to help you recognize when you need to make game time adjustments.

When you have that physical feeling, your job is to immediately act on it.

It may take you some time to learn to immediately act on it like it did me.

Persist to act on it, even if it's a week later. Persist to close the gap on how long it takes you.

57

Persist, persist, and persist in monitoring your feelings, and have the courage to change your thought.

You may be completely justified in anger. You may be justified in frustration. Simply ask yourself if being angry, frustrated, or whatever state you are in is a benefit or a negative, and rather than judge your feelings, simply observe them.

Have the expectation that you will continue to get better, and better, and better at this exercise.

Having the expectation of being perfect at controlling your ego will only cause you to let yourself down.

There will come the time where your ego shows up unexpectedly and catches you off guard, so the challenge remains: how long will it take you to regain control?

Say "Change" out loud or find something similar to help you reset and regain control.

Give yourself permission to learn and grow. Don't focus your thought on how often your ego is besting you; focus on the success you are having by recognizing when, where, how, and why your ego is trying to steal the show, and by seeing that this recognition is a complete success in helping you stay in the present. ⚲

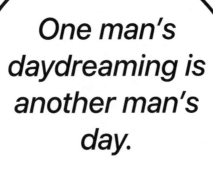

One man's daydreaming is another man's day.

Grey Livingston

 # CHAPTER 7

WHEN WAS THE LAST TIME YOU LET YOURSELF DAYDREAM?

Now that you've gotten a glimpse of what it's like to regain control of your thoughts, let's go further!

The next exercise will help you become the master of your thinking and take back control of ALL of your thoughts.

When you wake up and you start thinking of problems, you'll be much more adept at how to reset your mind, clear the problems out quickly, and have the solutions come to you effortlessly.

Soon, it'll be automatic behavior for you to upgrade your thinking wherever you are: at lunch, before a meeting, after an argument, etc.

You can learn to restart your mind at any time of day in any environment.

Sometimes, it might seem like the more complex a matter is, the more challenging it'll be — other times, it's the simplest things that might prove to be the toughest. What I'm about to share with you is simple...so simple that you might not even do it. Be mindful of your ego fooling you into thinking that because it is easy to do, you do not really need to practice the exercise.

This suggestion is vital: take time today to zone out.

Restart.
Readjust.
Optimize.
Maximize.

Relax, and drift off. Give your ego and conscious mind a break and allow your subconscious mind to go to work.

61

It may be for five minutes, thirty minutes or longer. The length of time doesn't matter; it's simply the practice of doing it that matters.

This exercise is very helpful when all the "recordings" start playing inside your head. It's an immediate way to shut them off and re-start your mind.

If you're like me you may be thinking, "I'm not sure if I can shut my thoughts off."

The truth is that you can't shut your thoughts off. You're always thinking. The purpose of this exercise is to turn your thinking over to your subconscious mind.

I have thoughts that come into my head, especially if I am spending more than a few minutes doing this exercise, and you will too. When I become aware of these thoughts, I observe them and ask myself, "Why am I having this thought?" The false thoughts disappear, and the true thoughts stay or evolve into something else.

This exercise is perfect whenever I have a challenging problem or I'm working to come up with an idea for one of my clients. Before I start the exercise, I tell myself, "Solve this problem," and then zone out.

This exercise requires discipline and persistence, and I want you to give it a shot, regardless of your fear of not being able to. Again, the length of time does not matter, the practice of the exercise is the main objective. The more you practice, the longer you will be able to perform the exercise.

If you are not able to quiet your mind, take a break and try another time. Stick with it. You will be able to learn how to do this sooner than you think if you will simply stick with it and keep trying.

I used to believe I needed to stay busy all the time, and that if work was not being completed quickly, money was being lost. I became more and more busy. Some days it felt like I could not get ahead, that I was never going to succeed.

I also used to go to sleep with what seemed like thousands of thoughts racing through my head uncontrolled, so I can tell you that it is indeed possible to quiet the thousands of thoughts racing through your head. It's also possible to easily become relaxed.

Daydreaming is a great skill to have when you want to re-start your thought.

When we're young, we easily indulge in playful and imaginative thinking, because that's our natural state of being. We're designed to be curious, so that we can learn how to become ourselves.

Then, we grow up, go to school, get a job, and are taught to fall in line by working hard, hustling, and trying to make as much money as possible.

If we don't press pause on this process and allow ourselves to enjoy the unfolding of our lives, then we'll simply get caught in the rat race of living by someone else's priorities and values.

When I learned to observe my thought without judgment, I began to experience true freedom.

It is my desire for you to experience this same freedom, and so I happily share my experience in how I arrived here with you.

Think of this as you just listening. You're not responsible for contributing to the conversation. You're just here to listen. It doesn't matter whether your eyes are open or not. The most important aspect will be starting this in an environment where you feel safe and comfortable.

If you're having a particular challenge that is consuming your thought, tell yourself, "Solve this problem for me," before starting. That's all you have to do.

1. Lie flat on a couch, bed or even the floor.
2. Raise your right arm six inches to a foot in the air and let it fall.
3. Do this a second time and then repeat with your left arm, your right leg, and finish with your left leg.
4. This will help you become relaxed enough where you can zone out for a few minutes.

This is one of my favorite things to do before my office opens in the morning and during lunch.

When I first learned this exercise, all would be quiet in my mind for about 30 seconds to a minute, and then, BAM! I would start thinking about what I could lose, which would typically be focused on an active client of my advertising business canceling their services with me.

I'd forget to observe my thoughts and instead would judge them. And what usually accompanies judgment? A sentence. I'd sentence myself, as weak, incapable of success, and filled with fear.

The only way to break this kind of thinking was to stop judging my thoughts.

I had to learn how to stop judgment in its tracks and observe.

I started to ask myself, "What thought am I thinking right now? Is there any benefit to thinking this? Does this thought help me? Is thinking this way hurting me? How can I improve this thought?"

I asked questions like these and observed the answers. Truth withstands all observation. Anything untrue does not withstand the forces of observation. Observation always reveals the truth.

What a revelation!

By asking the right questions, we have a better opportunity to receive the right answers.

The first few times you do this exercise it may take you a few minutes to get there. If it takes you a full hour, that is ok. This is not a contest. The main objective is for you to learn and know that you can do it.

Once you achieve turning off your ego driven and conscious thought, you may stay there for only a few seconds, and that's fine. If you stay there for five seconds today, you should be able to stay for 10 seconds or longer tomorrow. Do not try to go there. Just go there and allow it to happen.

If it doesn't happen right away, don't worry.

Allow it to happen.

The less effort you give in turning off your intentional thought the better. You will find that when you begin to let go and stop trying to think or not think (trying to manage your thought), it will happen naturally.

In summary, zone out. Daydream without a focus on any thought. Purposefully think of nothing. So right now, take a moment and go into the zone. You can even say, "Go into the zone or zone out" if that helps.

Go there now.

CHAPTER SUMMARY

I have learned that the best thing to do when I am feeling busy or rushed is to purposefully slow down. Often, as if by magic, the answers to problems have come to me after taking a break from thinking about them.

Be present in every moment and observe without judgment. You need not form an opinion, good or bad, on any thought that comes up. When you notice a thought, simply ask yourself these types of questions:

> Why am I thinking this?
> What is this thought about?
> How does this thought help me?
> Does this thought hurt me?
> Is there any benefit to thinking this?

The first few times I observed my thought like this I felt different. I felt different because I was having a new experience with my thought. I wasn't used to it. It was new. I also had to learn how to get past the fear of a new feeling to be able to observe my thoughts without judging them.

The only way to learn this was to persist in honestly observing the thoughts without judgment. If I did judge a thought, I would ask myself, "Is it better to judge this thought or observe it? Would you like to observe it now?"

The strength of my belief of needing to judge myself and my thinking quickly weakened when I started to ask myself these questions. Today, I still find myself judging my thoughts (it is likely that I always will), but I am able to recognize this quickly and move to a state of observation. I know today that it is not my responsibility or right to judge.

We are to observe and learn.

The easiest way to learn how to observe is to start observing. Do it right now. It does not work well when you think of observing your thought as a mechanism that acts like a burglar alarm. You cannot expect notifications and alerts. You have to make the decision to consciously observe your thought.

When should you do this exercise? NOW.

Find a comfortable environment and say to yourself, "Zone out, or go into the zone." Find what works best for you. You will also find that as you learn to control your mind, you will be able to perform this work in nearly any environment.

Learning that I could "get into the zone" I have been able to progress to a relaxed state where I do not have to go through raising and dropping my arms and legs every time. I can be sitting down or standing and produce the same effect. I have learned to do it on demand as needed, and you can too.

However long or short of time you were able to do this exercise, keep at it.

Remember, any resistance to this is generated by you. You are creating resistance by allowing your ego to influence your thought processes. When you experience resistance, remind yourself that you are the one creating this resistance and choose to observe only when it happens.

Do not judge yourself. The more time you spend in observation, the more you strengthen your consciousness and take power away from your ego.

If you are really struggling, a great time of day to practice is right before going to sleep. Think only positive thoughts and let yourself drift into deep sleep. Do it over and over every night. You may wake up to find you had one of your best night's sleep in a long time.

TRAINING EXERCISE

When you practice turning off all deliberate thought, you're able to be more purposeful in what next step will serve you best in your life.

Can you have thoughts without judging yourself?

Can you give yourself the freedom of playing with your ideas?

The first few times you do this exercise, it may take you a few minutes to quiet your restless mind.

In fact, it may even take you an hour or more.

That's okay.

It's not a contest and the less effort you put into it, the better.

You'll find that you can begin to let go and stop "trying" to think.

The more you can let go and the more relaxed you are, the more you can get into the zone of daydreaming ways to play and enjoy yourself, so you have space to choose more deliberate thoughts that do indeed serve you.

Perform this relaxation exercise as many times each day as you would like. Make sure to have a consistent time that you do it at least once every day, no matter what your schedule is:

Lie flat on a couch, bed or even the floor.

Raise your right arm six inches to a foot in the air and let it fall. Do this a second time.

Raise your left arm six inches to a foot in the air and let it fall. Do this a second time.

Raise your right leg six inches to a foot in the air and let it fall. Do this a second time.

Raise your left leg six inches to a foot in the air and let it fall. Do this a second time.

A great question to ask yourself before drifting off is, "What is the greatest expression of myself?"

GO DEEPER

Remember persistence? This is not a one-time exercise. It is a daily exercise for the rest of your life if you are serious about keeping control of your thought. Here are some tips on making sure you remember to do the exercises daily:

Schedule time on your calendar specifically for these exercises. This gives you a notification, a reminder, every day to do the exercises.

Place thought provokers around your daily routine. What are thought provokers? They are simple objects that are visibly out of place, designed to make yourself stop and think. I use golf tees and place them in odd places. I place them in a different location every few days, so I do not get used to them being in the same spot. ⅄

68

Success is not a matter of mastering subtle, sophisticated theory but rather of embracing common sense with uncommon levels of discipline and persistence.

Patrick Lencioni

 # CHAPTER 8

RECOGNIZE SUCCESS

Often, when on a spiritual or personal development path, we can become so focused on what we want to have, that we continually try to improve with bigger and better outcomes, failing to recognize how far we have come. This can be very frustrating, especially with success-minded people. If we're trying to improve and build bigger and better things, shouldn't we be positively focused on those goals? Shouldn't it be a good thing to focus on improving?

Yes, absolutely it is a good thing to improve. However, when we fail to recognize our successes as we make them, we open up the door for failure to walk in and pull the rug right out from underneath us.

Opportunities for failure increase when we fail to recognize our successes.

You have heard the expression, "Rome wasn't built in a day." Great achievements take time to evolve. Our culture of immediate gratification has the potential to hold each and every one of us prisoner; able to set goals, but never achieve them because we expect our goals to evolve with the same speed as online shopping. You can't buy success, and success is not given away.

You have to create success.

There is always a price to be paid, and the good news is you have every capability in paying the price. The price? Everlasting persistence.

The greater your desire is, the more persistence and faith you will need to back it with. So how do we make something successful if we cannot attain it right away? Recognize movement toward your goal as success.

Recognize every success as a building block to the next success, great or small in your life.

Think of each success like a Lego block. You start with one, but when you add another the size of the total object grows. Each piece added changes the shape and mass of the object. If you are building a castle, you cannot add the finishing flag without the tower underneath it, and you cannot have a tower without first building a solid foundation.

Every small success you have adds to the size and effect of your overall success. The greater achievement is dependent on the foundational achievements, the small successes.

Everything you do can be made into a successful act.

How can everything you do be made into a successful act? It is possible because you are completely in control of your conception of success. Your successes are only successes because you have the belief, **the conception**, of their success.

Once you understand the power your conceptions have in creating all the experiences in your life, you will be exceptionally diligent in making sure your conceptions are exactly the way you want them to be.

Take the color red for example. The properties of the color red are commonly accepted around the world. Red is one of the first colors children learn, but what if you took a child and taught him from birth that the color you have the conception of as red is named blue?

This child would know what you call a red rose to be a blue rose. A red firetruck would be a blue firetruck. A red apple would be a blue apple. The child's conception of the color you call red would always be blue.

Consider this scenario: This child never has their conception of the color red challenged, not one time. The child grows up always knowing it to be blue.

On this person's 18th birthday you are the first one to present the fact that the color the child has been calling blue for 18 years really is named and accepted by the rest of the world as red.

Do you think this person would immediately change their conception of red and agree with you? It is highly unlikely. Even presenting the most convincing evidence in the world, you would be arguing against 18 years of programming. Would this person's conception of the color red be wrong? It would be wrong to you, but not wrong to the new adult.

Your conception of things is all that matters.

Now, you are going to add your conceptions of all things as thought you are constantly monitoring. Your job is to turn every conception of your experiences into a successful one. Everything you do must be successful for this to fully work. Everything.

Experiences you previously defined as failures, problems, and frustrations now must be turned into successes. In everything you do success really is there and finding and recognizing it will start to pay off big time.

I have experienced my fair share of "setbacks" in my marketing business. One of the first really painful ones was losing a million-dollar account. I did not see the silver lining anywhere. It was a massive failure in my eyes. I dealt with it by doubling my personal sales efforts to make up for the loss in revenue, and it took my company over a year to recover.

A few years later I lost a half-million-dollar account. However, this time it was a complete success. Here are three successes I immediately recognized:

1. The potential loss was predicted six months out and I had already replaced the revenue with two accounts.
2. I now had a perfect opportunity to re-allocate internal resources to other markets.
3. The opportunity and timeline to move our headquarters to another market was accelerated by a full year.

Did I see success with this account 24/7 after losing it? No. I still had moments of frustration, and my ego had plenty of ideas to share with me. The difference was that I was prepared to flood those negative thoughts away with positive ones.

I changed my conception of what many would consider a failure into a success. The only effort required by me was monitoring my thought and having the will to mentally turn failure into success.

What was the actual effect of losing the half-million-dollar account? Financially, it was like nothing happened. There was no recovery period. My company actually continued to grow financially.

Emotionally, we are grateful for the work and wish our former client the best. We only have good things to say about them. Do you get where I'm going here on making every move a success?

But what if something has really gone wrong in your life, something completely unexpected and out of your control, something horrible?

Admiral Chester Nimitz had a different conception of the Japanese attack on Pearl Harbor than anyone else when he was given a tour of the destruction on Christmas Day, 1941. The following is taken from *Reflections on Pearl Harbor* by Admiral Chester Nimitz.

> When asked what Admiral Nimitz thought about the destruction he said, "The Japanese made three of the biggest mistakes an attack force could ever make, or God was taking care of America. Which do you think it was?"
>
> Shocked and surprised with the Admiral's answer, the reply was, "What do mean by saying the Japanese made the three biggest mistakes an attack force ever made?"
>
> Mistake number one: the Japanese attacked on Sunday morning. Nine out of every ten crewmen of those ships were ashore on leave. If those same ships had been lured to sea and been sunk--we would have lost 38,000 men instead of 3,800.
>
> Mistake number two: when the Japanese saw all those battleships lined in a row, they got so carried away sinking those battleships, they never once bombed our dry docks opposite those ships. If they had destroyed our dry docks, we would have had to tow every

one of those ships to America to be repaired. As it is now, the ships are in shallow water and can be raised. One tug can pull them over to the dry docks, and we can have them repaired and at sea by the time we could have towed them to America. And I already have crews ashore anxious to man those ships.

Mistake number three: every drop of fuel in the Pacific theater of war is in top of the ground storage tanks five miles away over that hill. One attack plane could have strafed those tanks and destroyed our fuel supply. That's why I say the Japanese made three of the biggest mistakes an attack force could make, or God was taking care of America.

America had just experienced an incredible tragedy, and Admiral Nimitz chose not to focus his energy on what had been lost, but on gratitude for what had been saved, thousands of lives, all the dry docks, and all the fuel.

Nature balances itself perfectly. With every disappointment, failure, and setback there is an equivalent seed of opportunity. You can find success and opportunity in everything you do, and when everything you do is successful, you can only be successful.

This is the magic formula that will deliver the really big stuff in your life. Where most people slip up is in failing to recognize what they already have by showing, experiencing, and expressing sincere gratitude for those things.

By only focusing on what we want to have and not being grateful for what we have achieved we run the risk of living in a state of want, always wishing we had more.

This is where gratitude comes into play. Gratitude is one of the greatest tools for growth. By actively expressing sincere gratitude for what we have, more and more and more is received.

Can you find a way to be grateful for everything in your life today, even finding ways to turn current disappointments into grateful opportunities?

CHAPTER SUMMARY

In nature the law of survival of the fittest rules. The strongest survive and the weak are consumed. Humans do not hunt each other physically; we hunt each other financially. We view the world with the ones having the most money ruling over all.

"Keeping up with the Joneses" is a bad habit. When we focus our attention on what everyone else has, we take our attention away from our blessings.

This creates a failure mentality because all you are looking at is what you don't have. And because all you are thinking about is what you don't have, you continue to experience more and more of "not having."

TRAINING EXERCISE

What are you grateful for? Really, truly grateful for?

Make a list where you're physically writing down what you appreciate.

Every day read your list aloud. Then, add to it.

By reading it aloud, you can feel your gratitude more intensely, and by spending about 15 seconds thinking about each one, you're propelling yourself forward in your day with positive thought.

Several pages are provided at the end of the book for you to write your gratitude list. I strongly encourage you to physically write your list down before putting it on a device like your phone or computer. Something magic happens when you write.

GO DEEPER

Let's say you buy a present for a friend on their birthday. You have the best intentions of them really enjoying it. You have it wrapped and take it to their birthday party, excited to see their surprise when your present is opened in front of everyone.

Your friend opens it, and as the paper is torn away you can't wait for their reaction. However, instead of being grateful when the present is opened, your friend looks up and says, "Oh? I thought you'd give me something nicer."

Your happy emotion of giving now feels like a punch in the gut.

Would you feel like giving this friend another present? Would you even come to the birthday party next year?

Now, put yourself in your friend's shoes, except look at everything in your life as presents you have been given. Can you be grateful for them, or do you feel like you've been shorted?

Your car is too old. Your house is too small. You're in a dead-end job. The example above of an ungrateful friend illustrates an unwillingness to give more. Is it fair for you expect to have more and better things when you look at everything in your life as not good enough?

The truth is that focusing on what you don't want or have only keeps what you don't want or have present. Look at everything in your life and how it can help you.

See how negative experiences have taught you valuable lessons. Be thankful for the relationships (good and bad) in your life and what they teach you. Be thankful for what you have and ask yourself what you can do to make them even better.

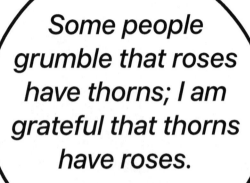

Some people grumble that roses have thorns; I am grateful that thorns have roses.

Alphonse Karr

Chapter 9

GRATITUDE

Gratitude is HUGE, and the practice of gratitude is equally as important as persistence. If it is so important, then why have I waited to until now to bring it up? If you are anything like me, your mind needed a little cleansing first.

I have understood the definition of gratitude, the quality of being thankful, from the first time I was introduced to it, but just because I understood it, does not mean that I knew how to apply it.

Real gratitude produces a good, physical feeling.

There is a big difference between saying "thank you" for something, and truly being grateful for it. Going through the motions saying "thank you" or "yes, I'm grateful for this or that" doesn't count as true gratitude unless you are experiencing a positive, emotional feeling with it.

I spent most of my life going through the motions of just saying "thanks." I even became so cynical at one point in my life that I looked at gratitude as weakness. I did not want to be obligated to anyone who had given me anything to be grateful for.

An experience that used to drive me crazy was receiving a gift I was not expecting. When this happened, I would look at it like "Great, now I have to get this person something in return," instead of thinking something like "What a nice surprise. I'm really grateful to have people in my life who think I'm worth giving a gift to."

My ego had complete control of my ability to experience gratitude. My ego convinced me that because of the mistakes I had made in my life, I did not deserve to receive anything good. This is why I waited until now to talk about gratitude. My ego was completely in the way of me experiencing gratitude. I had to regain control of my thinking before I could truly be grateful for anything.

Displaying an attitude of gratitude is the equivalent to having a blank check with no limit.

This is where you can put the instruction of "It is more blessed to give than to receive," Acts 20:35, to use. Gratitude combines the emotions of love and faith together, and when we sincerely give gratitude for what we have and desire to have in our lives, we receive it back, only multiplied. Gratitude is the secret sauce in making the karmic law perfectly work for you.

I used to limit myself by being competitive instead of grateful. Watching and participating in organized sports helped me develop an extremely competitive personality.

This competitive spirit became a part of my every day practice in my professional life. I looked at every competing business and their associates as the enemy. They were all threats to me, and because I kept an attitude of them being a threat, they naturally were a threat.

Competitors would say things about me or my company. Competitors would try to take away my business by offering different products and pricing. I could find a way to look at any move by competitors in my industry as an "attack."

I had zero gratitude for competitors, and any thought related to them was focused on how I could put them out of business. Looking at my competitors as the enemy didn't rid me of any. They actually grew in number and continued to be active and irritating.

Replacing competitiveness with gratitude.

When I discovered the book, *The Science of Getting Rich*, by Wallace D. Wattles, the idea of competitiveness being a negative practice was introduced to me. This went against everything I believed related to competition because I had always believed competition to be necessary. "Survival of the fittest" was how I had lived my entire life.

Fortunately, by the time I read this book I had developed the practice of re-reading and listening to materials over and over again. It took me at least

80

10 times of reading *The Science of Getting Rich* before I was willing to try not being competitive. My identity was rooted in competitiveness so just being willing to try a different way was significant.

I did not know I had been living with scales over my eyes, keeping me trapped and blinded from the truth for so long. When I became willing to replace competitiveness with gratitude, a new view of the world started to take shape.

I began to notice the undeniable abundance around me. Everything around me became plentiful. Trees, rocks, animals, water, food, shelter, entertainment, beautiful places, stars, everything...there was more than could be counted of all.

There was more available to me than I could possibly use, and through seeing the abundance around me I was able to know for sure that there was no need for competitiveness in my life.

Competing with others for the same "stuff" is a waste of time and energy. There is more than enough of everything for all of us to have and experience. If you are focusing your thought on what isn't in your life and how hard it is to get because you have to compete with others for it, guess what? You will get exactly that. You will constantly experience dis-satisfaction with your surroundings and others because you are always worried about them either taking from you or having more than you.

How do I look at competition now? My advertising business has a tremendous number of competitors who are constantly pursuing our clients. I used to be very frustrated and angry about this, but today I remain grateful for it. I can be grateful, because today, I have the conception that these companies help my company be better all around.

Competitors help me make sure my pricing is in line with the market. They make sure I am offering the most appropriate services. They push me to develop new services and products that are better for our clients. They keep my staff and I active in maintaining our personal relationships with our clients.

81

I know that there are a multitude of businesses ready to be a client of my company, so many available that I will never be able to reach them all. There is always plenty for me and every business in my category.

I don't look at these other businesses as competitors anymore but as peers who, along with me, are trying to help other businesses promote their products and services in the best way possible. We all have strengths and unique characteristics which have been given to and developed by us to help others.

If I have a client leave my company, I am grateful for the experience we were able to have in helping them. I'm grateful for the lessons we learned and the opportunity we will have to apply those lessons with the next client. I'm grateful that company has options to choose from in helping them with their goals.

We manage and give our clients what we believe to be the most exceptional service and marketing products available. We strive to bring new ideas to an ever-changing marketing world. We work very hard to become what our clients would consider an invaluable partner in their business.

We make every relationship successful. This is the big difference in how we think today. Client, internal, vendor, competitor...ALL relationships are successful today, and allow us to grow and evolve. Maintaining an attitude of gratitude allows this to be as easy as breathing. It just happens today because we know there is more than enough for all of us.

Making everything a success helps foster and maintain an attitude of gratitude for all that is happening.

CHAPTER SUMMARY

Think of your body like an electromagnet. For an electromagnet to work there must be both a magnet and electricity. Unlike a permanent magnet, the strength of an electromagnet can easily be changed by increasing or decreasing the amount of electric current that flows through it. The poles of an electromagnet can even be reversed by reversing the flow of electricity.

Your thoughts are the electricity and your feelings are the magnet. You must have both thought and feeling for your electromagnet to work. Your thoughts (positive or negative) activate the power of the magnet. Stronger emotions increase, and weaker emotions decrease the magnet's power.

The poles of your electromagnet attract by the nature of your thoughts. Positive thoughts attract good things. Negative thoughts attract bad things.

Thought alone will not attract what you desire. Thinking and not feeling is like trying to make the electromagnet work without the magnet. You must have emotional thought. As you review your gratitude list in the exercise below, **FEEL your gratitude.**

Go back to the exact moment these things on your gratitude list came into your life and remember how you felt. Feel those feelings again as your read through your list.

TRAINING EXERCISE

Review your gratitude list.

Spend a few seconds on each thing you wrote down and visualize your gratitude for it. The idea is for you to physically feel the gratitude you have. Spend as much time as you like on each item.

Ask yourself if you are willing to replace competitiveness with gratitude.

Write down one item on your gratitude list that you are currently competitive with and turn it into something you can be grateful for.

GO DEEPER

If you are living your life in a state of want, it can be really difficult to shift that state into an attitude of gratitude. Could it be that you are physically addicted to your emotions?

Why does a heroin addict keep using heroin? Because of the feeling produced by the drug. The addict's body influences actions by producing feelings to urge the addict to use more heroin.

Emotions produce chemical reactions in the body, and we can become addicted to them just like a heroin addict gets addicted to heroin. Our bodies can become addicted to the feelings emotions produce.

When you have those moments of, "Everything was going right, and then it just crashed and burned," time after time, ask yourself these questions.

Is it possible I have programmed myself for this result? Am I creating the same feelings of failure and frustration over and over? What were my feelings before I crashed and burned?

Actively monitor your feelings. Positive feelings feel loose and relaxed. Negative feelings are tight and constricted. When you feel tight and constricted, ask yourself what you are thinking. Is this thought positive or negative? Is it helping or hurting me?

Just observe the answers. Don't judge yourself if the thought is negative. Simply change it. Feel good. If you're struggling to feel good, PERSIST and dive deep into your gratitude list. Add to your gratitude list and be present with everything that is right and beautiful in your life. ☘

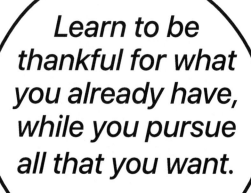

Learn to be
thankful for what
you already have,
while you pursue
all that you want.

Jim Rohn

 # CHAPTER 10
CREATING GRATITUDE

Do you believe that both a positive and negative thought can co-exist at the same time? Give thinking both these thoughts at the same time a few efforts. Do it at least three times:

Positive thought: I am successful.
Negative thought: I am a failure.

Remember, think both of these thoughts together at the same time, at least 3 times.

What did you experience? Were you able to have both those thoughts at the same time?

It is impossible to hold both a negative and positive thought in your mind simultaneously. This should be proof enough on why you should always be working to Think A Better Thought™.

Now do the same exercise with statements of gratitude. Give these two thoughts your attention and observe if it is possible to hold both of them in your thought at the same time. Think of a person you are fond of with both of these thoughts:

Grateful thought: I appreciate having you in my life.
Ungrateful thought: I hate you. Why are you in my life?

Were you able to hold both thoughts in your mind at the same time? More importantly, how did you feel when you had the thought of wanting a person you are fond of to be out of your life?

Now restate the grateful thought, "I appreciate having you in my life," while you hold that person's image in your mind. Notice the difference in feeling? Think about the mental, physical and spiritual effects feelings like this related to things you are not grateful for have on you. Ask yourself if it would be of benefit for you to have more gratitude in your life.

By supplying yourself with an abundance of positive thoughts, you can help wash away any negative thoughts you'll come across in life. If you want to acquire the use of having a blank check with no limit, the skill of gratitude must be mastered.

Again, a great place to start is your gratitude list. Creating a gratitude list gives you a perfect go-to tool when you're feeling annoyed or frustrated, experiencing hopelessness, or feeling lost in anxiety. This is why you started creating a gratitude list earlier. Gratitude immediately turns your experience into a positive one.

Gratitude works just like persistence. You have to do it to get more of it.

You cannot think your way into persistence or gratitude; you just have to be persistent and grateful. You either are or you aren't. It is that simple. So why is it so hard for some people to have an attitude of gratitude? The answer is they lack persistence in maintaining it.

If you have ever had your back adjusted by a chiropractor, then you understand how muscle memory can pull the adjustment out of alignment. Sometimes, particularly if you have been out of alignment for a while, it takes several treatments to keep the adjustment in place. The muscle memory wants to keep pulling your bones back out of alignment.

The same holds true with your mind. If you have the mental muscle memory of being highly competitive like I was, or you get easily offended for example, you can't expect to completely turn off this way of thinking. It is unreasonable to expect these thoughts not to pop up again. Eventually, we all let our guard down and slip. We get "hangry" and have a fit. When this happens make a mental adjustment.

Your job is to get your thinking back in line. You are 100% responsible for making the adjustment because only you truly know your thoughts.

88

Again, this is why you started a gratitude list earlier. Your gratitude list should never end. Always keep working on it and adding to it. You can have any kind of gratitude list you like, and you can have as many as you want. You can have one, big master list or several lists. I like to keep mine on my phone, so I can review or add to it any time I want.

The gratitude list is no good if it is not reviewed daily and infused with positive emotion. The practice of reviewing it daily has more than one benefit. In addition to putting your mind in a completely positive state, reviewing your gratitude list helps you start turning everything into something you can be grateful for.

As you review your gratitude list daily, you will begin to add more and more to the list. You will start to recall things you did not realize you were grateful for. You will become so accustomed to looking for what to be grateful for that eventually you will find gratitude in everything around you.

You will recognize the feeling of ungratefulness and want to rid yourself of it immediately, and you will do this by either going straight to your gratitude list, or you will be able to transform your ungratefulness to gratitude with that person, place, or thing within moments.

Examples of creating gratitude.

The first line with each example is the ungrateful thought, and the second, in bold, is the transformation to gratitude. These are examples to help you start thinking how you can transform anything you do not desire into gratitude. You'll write down a few of your own at the end of the chapter.

I can't believe it's raining. I wanted to take my dog to the park today.
I love being a safe place for my dog when he gets scared by thunder.

This waitress is so slow. I'm sure she's going to mess our order up.
Isn't it great to have a little more time to relax and enjoy some conversation before we eat?

We have the worst neighbors. Their kids are in and out of their house all day long.

One good thing about our neighbor's kids is that they are sure to keep away anyone interested in robbing the neighborhood. They're always in and out!

I can't believe it's Monday already. How do I escape this job?
I'm really grateful for what I've learned at my job. I feel ready for new opportunities to learn even more and can't wait to find them!

CHAPTER SUMMARY

As you go about your day start thinking about how you can maintain an attitude of gratitude every step of the way. An effective tool you can use is a thought provoker.

A thought provoker is a physical object used to jog your memory. One of the first versions of a thought provoker I can remember being shown was to tie a string around your finger to remind yourself of a task. Use what works best for you.

Pick an object that is unique and unordinary. I like using something small enough to fit in my pocket. Place it where you will visibly notice it, where it is out of place. When you notice it, this is your reminder to practice gratitude. Make sure to change where your thought provoker is placed so you do not get used to it.

TRAINING EXERCISE

There are two routes you can take with your thoughts, one is positive, the other is negative.

For example, let's say you are in rush hour traffic on the freeway and get cut off by someone shortcutting a long line you have waited in to exit. They don't even use their blinker and nearly swipe your left fender.

You immediately lay on the horn, flash your high beams, and make

90

gestures with your hands while you yell out, "Idiot! Who the hell are you! You *$@!@*#!@*!!!!"

You inch up as close as you can to their bumper doing everything you can without hitting their car to let them know that they are a terrible driver!

OR...

You slow down and let them move ahead a bit. You take a breath and are thankful they didn't cause any damage to your car that would have caused a longer delay.

You can be grateful that you don't have to feel rushed like they are. You can be grateful that you do not have that person's burden. They might have a family member or friend in need.

You can send them a positive thought that they won't need to be rushed and be thankful that you are in control.

Think about something that easily annoys or offends you. Write that down on the lines below.

_____

_____

Now take the subject above and create a way you can be grateful for it. Don't cheat yourself on this. It is easy to be sarcastic with your gratitude when you first learn this. Sarcasm and gratitude do not exist with one another. Work this until you are really grateful for some portion, benefit or lesson of the subject above. Use the lines below.

_____

_____

GO DEEPER

Have you ever heard of a gratitude rock? A gratitude rock is a thought provoker. The only difference is you keep it in your pocket and don't set it around your home or office. When you pull it out or place it into your pocket, you are to be reminded to think of something you are grateful for.

Find a rock that is just the right size to easily fit into your pocket or purse. I like to use rocks that I have found on our family vacations. If I'm struggling to think of something to be grateful for, I can always go back to a scenic view or great experience we had in the place my rock is from. ⌄

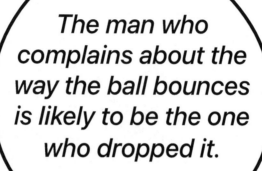

The man who complains about the way the ball bounces is likely to be the one who dropped it.

Lou Holtz

CHAPTER 11

THE ULTIMATE ENEMY

It's easy to place blame on other people, places, or things — I'd say, I became an expert at it.

I have experienced all types of failures and setbacks in my life. Most have been caused by me, but other significant ones have been caused by those closely associated with me.

I was sexually abused as a child. My life has been threatened and I've been mugged. I've had my house broken into. I have been mocked and made fun of in school. I've been fired twice.

So what.

There's nothing unique about my failures and setbacks. Everyone experiences them. We all get "screwed over" by someone else eventually. Your choice of conception about negative experiences is what matters.

Are you using each experience to advance you toward achieving your goal, into becoming a smarter, more productive person? Or, are you keeping the experience of your pain or loss alive with resentment and thoughts of revenge? Resentment can only be looked at in one way.

Resentment is the ultimate enemy and must be destroyed.

Right now, you may be telling yourself, "Whew! No resentments here. Let's move forward!"

Before we "move forward," let me ask you one question: Do you know a "son-of-a-bitch?" Maybe you know two...possibly three or four...more?

Let's start with the "SOBs," they're the easy ones to pick out, and they don't necessarily have to be a person. If you're resentful with the government for how high your taxes are, then the government just might be an SOB in your life. If you constantly dread your morning commute to work because of how long it takes, your commute could be an SOB. Another might be a co-worker who leaves their dirty dishes in the office sink for someone else to clean.

The point is to pick out something or someone you can easily see yourself having a resentment toward, so we can find out just how well that resentment is working for you.

First, recall when the experience happened that created your resentment with this person, place, or thing. How long ago did it occur? Now ask yourself this question:

Am I experiencing that event right now?

You may be resentful of it now, but the undeniable truth is that the experience is in the past. You only experienced it in your past. All of it happened and cannot be changed.

So, this negative experience that you have no power to ever change, an experience completely in your past...you are choosing to keep alive... essentially re-living the experience over and over again with your resentment. How fun and productive does resentment sound now?

Resentment is completely negative and can become so powerful that it blinds us to everything good. It is impossible for resentment to add anything positive in our lives.

Replace resentment with gratitude.

By transforming and transmuting the energy behind the things you hate, you can remove their power over you. You can surrender to them. You can learn from them. You can start to make them work with you instead of against you.

When you think of a past pain ask yourself, "Did blaming someone or something else help me in the end or, did it actually cause more pain?"

WHY did you blame?

Observe your answers with no judgment.

In 2008, my wife and I were approached by a competitor to merge with his company. Our company was still very small, just Dedee and me, and she was part-time. Merging was an opportunity to have staff right away and start working on more accounts.

I didn't put much research into it at all, and jumped right in.

I started to evaluate the business more closely after the merger and realized, "We've got some things we need to fix." However, my partner was not interested in changing the way he had done business for the past 35+ years.

I continued to be direct and persistent about my desire to make changes, and this caused enough tension that we mutually agreed it would be best to split the company up and go our separate ways. Nearly a year to the date of the original merger, the company was dissolved, and my wife and I formed a new company, SDB Creative Group.

That's the short story. Splitting caused some financial pain for me.

My partner claimed I owed the company $30,000. I couldn't believe this at first. If I really believed I owed $30,000, I would have paid it without question, but I felt the math was way off.

We went back and forth on the amount of money he was wanting, and I soon realized $30,000 was the price to pay for leaving. Paying this money made me so irate that I couldn't think one good thing about him, except for the fact that I no longer had to work with him. I felt deceived that I had to buy my way out of this deal. The resentment I had for him motivated me to work faster, harder, longer.

My new company grew, and his company continued to operate successfully from what I could tell. What he didn't know was how much time and energy I wasted resenting him.

I enjoyed success, but I really enjoyed it if I thought I was doing better than he was. I measured the success my company had against his all the time. All I wanted to do was beat him. I wanted him to see how big my company had become and have him regret his decision to not let me do things how I wanted to when we were partners.

He passed away in 2016, and I was still so resentful that I didn't even attend his funeral. "He brought it on himself," is what I thought. Then I realized that everything I was mad at him for, I've also done.

I came to realize that the bad you see in other people is the bad you need to work on within yourself — you can't see it unless you already have it.

That's when I started asking myself, "What good is it doing me to hold onto this resentment? How is this resentment helping me get what I want? Is this resentment helping or hurting me?" I realized this resentment held zero benefits for me, and I needed to change my thinking and state of mind related to it.

The solution was transforming the resentment to gratitude. It was uncomfortable at first, but after realizing the benefits of holding gratitude for him instead of resentment, I wish I had done it the day I gave him the $30,000.

I asked myself one simple question, "How can I be grateful for this relationship instead of resentful?" The answer didn't immediately pop into my head, but it did come. Here are the thoughts I was given in response to my question:

I learned how to staff an office for an advertising agency.

I learned about a part of the advertising industry I had no experience with before.

My clients thought enough of me to stay with me before, during, and after the merger.

I wasn't flooded with positive aspirations for this person when I asked the question, "How can I be grateful for this relationship instead of resentful," but I was given enough to shift my attitude about him to gratitude instead of resentment. Today I rarely give the merger experience a thought unless I am telling a story about our company's history.

Our egos fuel the practice of blaming others.

When we point blame away from ourselves, we remove that sense of empowered agency that gives us the opportunity for growth. We shortchange ourselves from the opportunity to evolve.

We try to use this passive aggressive shortcut to force getting what we want by manipulating and blaming other people, places, or things instead of taking ownership of everything that's happened in our lives.

While it may feel like temporary relief in the moment, this blaming way of thinking actually keeps us trapped. What ultimately happens is that you give up your power to grow, change, and clear your mind when you blame others.

So, let me ask you now...

How many emotional crutches, excuses, resentments are you using today?

Is it easy for you to blame someone, something, or someplace else for your problems?

Here is where it may get a little tough for you. Be alert for your ego working against you. I'm going to challenge you here. Start by thinking about past times when you blamed someone for something in your life. Do you still hold resentment for this experience, or can you find gratitude with it?

Eventually you are going to have to really dig deep and find all of them, even the ones that had a long-lasting sting or still hurt. The tough part ahead is going to be in mastering your ability to be honest with yourself related to your feelings. Your ego can easily use past pain to manipulate you into thinking you are justified in blaming someone or something else for failure, disappointment, or pain.

If you can't get there right away, don't give up. If you feel like it is too hard, start with something that is more minor to warm up with, like being cut off in traffic. You are learning what tools are available to you and how to use them. The more you learn about them and how to use them, the better you will become, and you'll be able to take on the tough stuff with full confidence.

I used to feel like I wasted years of my life over numerous meaningless experiences that were filled with resentment, anger, fury, and hatred. Today, I can see these experiences weren't wasted, but they have become part of my story and were necessary for me to be able to help others going through similar experiences.

Find a way to be grateful for all your experiences and set yourself free.

CHAPTER SUMMARY

Ask yourself if it helps or hurts you to have resentment in your life. Resentment does not have to be about you. It can simply start with resentment in general. As you continue to observe resentment in your life you will see that it magically disappears.

Here's how:

The secret is observation and not judgment of your resentment. Judgment creates an effect resulting in a sentence. We do not desire to sentence ourselves any longer. We desire to grow, to experience true freedom. Observation is the secret to making this happen.

All things true in this life will survive all observation. This is the truth. A truth in your life will withstand all observation. Anything in your life that is not true will not survive. A non-truth cannot survive observation. This includes resentment.

Ask yourself, "Is there any benefit in keeping a resentment against this person, place or thing? Is it helping me or is it hurting me? Will this resentment get me what I want?" Observe the answer. Do not judge.

TRAINING EXERCISE

For today, how can you take a look at an experience in the past, one that you've been harboring? Look at it from a different angle where you quit giving ownership to people who've done things TO you and instead, claim your power back by allowing yourself to know you are strong enough to take responsibility and now choose to let it go.

When you notice your resentments, ask yourself:

Why am I thinking of this resentment?

What is this resentment really about?

How does this resentment help me?

Does this resentment hurt me?

Is there any benefit to having this resentment?

How can I replace this resentment with gratitude?

Now, the secret to all this is not having judgment for yourself in the observation and answering of these questions.

Judgment creates an effect resulting in a confining sentence, and our true purpose is to feel completely free. Observe without judgment and free yourself.

GO DEEPER

I have wasted many hours of my life carrying resentment. There has been one person in particular who has stood at the front of my resentment line. This person has carefully disguised their identity and my resentment of them for many years. Only when I accepted that my best thinking had given me the exact life that I was experiencing did I learn the true identity of who I had been resenting, even hating, for much of my life.

Who was it?

It was me.

I had been my most cunning enemy. I had secretly been trying to self-sabotage myself nearly every step of the way. This is completely crazy thinking. Why would I ever do this to myself?

Did resenting myself have any benefit for me? No. When I asked myself this question and truly observed it, the resentment vanished. It dissolved, vaporized into thin air.

I have learned through observing others that I am not alone in resenting myself.

Most people have a veiled disgust with themselves. Why do we waste so much time being angry and resentful at ourselves? Who could possibly come up with such an argument that it would ever be correct to be internally resentful?

The only explanation is our egos.

Our egos rage, fearful of change. Our egos bring up every failure, embarrassment and disappointment against us. Our egos try to convince us that there is something wrong with us, something that is no good.

Is this the truth? Absolutely not! It is the furthest from the truth that can be. If you feel like you will not be able to gain freedom from resenting yourself, have no fear, you can and will.

Ask yourself if you have an internal resentment. You may need to ask yourself this question several times before you realize an answer. If you have any doubt at all, continue to ask the question.

If you do discover you have a resentment with yourself, continue with these questions and only observe.

Why am I thinking of this resentment?

What is this resentment really about?

How does this resentment help me?

Does this resentment hurt me?

Is there any benefit to having this resentment?

How can I replace this resentment with gratitude? ⚰

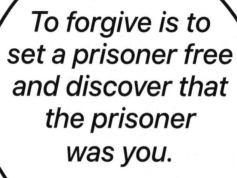

*To forgive is to
set a prisoner free
and discover that
the prisoner
was you.*

Lewis B. Smedes

CHAPTER 12
PRACTICE FORGIVENESS

You're now standing on the real, true path to success. You have begun to explore practices that will help you take back your thinking and STAY in control.

If you're really ready to catapult yourself forward, then here's the skill that'll truly launch you ahead: **PRACTICE FORGIVENESS.**

Forgiveness and releasing the need for blame go hand-in-hand.

A lot of us have had experiences where we feel like we're 100% the victim. Let's be honest, some people can be really nasty and do bad things.

When I first started practicing forgiveness on a more regular basis, it was exceptionally hard, and I also actually didn't feel much of a positive difference.

It wasn't until I began to explore more aspects of spirituality that I realized forgiveness was only a word that I was using — my resentment remained.

I learned that I actually didn't know HOW to forgive someone fully. It was a new skill I needed to acquire. And, here's how I did it:

Look at your life like it's one, big trip, a grand vacation. On this trip, you don't need any baggage, because everything is provided for you along the way: food, clothing, shelter, entertainment, etc.

However, if you'd like to carry some baggage, and bring items from one destination to the next, you may. You can choose any type of baggage you desire, and there's only one requirement for the baggage: You can't store it; your baggage must stay with you ALL the time.

No one can help you.

Everywhere you go on your vacation in life, your bags must also go with you.

If you go to the bathroom, your bags go with you.

If you go out to eat, your bags go too.

When you go to bed, your bags are in bed with you.

Every second you spend on your vacation all your bags must be right there with you.

You can have as many bags as you want, so long as they stay with you.

You've likely taken a trip before, seen someone at a hotel or convention center, where they're dragging one or more bags with them...they're struggling, even fighting to keep their bags from turning over.

It doesn't look fun at all and I usually think, "I'm sure glad that's not me."

Well, when it comes to being unable to forgive others, this same analogy applies — we're all dragging our bags to the next destination, slowing ourselves down, feeling weighed down by the effort of having to manage all this "stuff."

If you'll allow the pun, let's unpack what our bags really represent.

They represent our RESENTMENTS.

When you allow resentment to exist in your mind, you're allowing lack and poverty into your life.

Why?

Because resentment can literally be redefined as what you lack in your life. Why else would you be resentful of anything? It's usually because someone else has something you don't, or someone's wronged you out of something you think you should've had.

So, on this vacation of your life, you can either keep adding bags by picking up one resentment after another, then another, then another, and another... or you can stop.

You can make a choice right now to drop the hundreds of pounds of crap you've been dragging around. Do you really want this heaviness to be part of your everyday life?

Stop.

Take a moment.

Imagine for a moment that you're trying to keep up with HUNDREDS of bags. What does this feel like for you? Are you exhausted? Are you actually able to enjoy your trip, or are you so worried about keeping tabs on everything that you can't?

Have you ever held onto something so tightly and for so long that you physically had to pry your fingers off of it? Well, that's how holding onto resentment can feel.

Sometimes we can hold onto something for so long that it becomes part of our identity. The longer we hold on to resentment the harder it is to let it go and when we do allow ourselves to let it go, we usually have a cramping, aching sensation.

This "mental cramping" often causes us to wonder if we've made a mistake, and our programmed mental muscle memory wants to go through the motion of picking the resentment back up and continue holding onto it.

You're moving away from crazy thinking and self-sabotage, but you're also susceptible to bad mental muscle memory. If you are anything like me, it may be really hard to truly forgive someone and let a resentment go. The only person who will ever know if you have truly forgiven is you.

If you have experienced this same problem, I have a travel tip for you, and in fact, this golden nugget has allowed me to set down resentments completely and walk away from them forever.

What is the greatest revenge? Forgiveness.

If you're open to it, it's time to shift your perspective a little to see that forgiveness can be the best form of "revenge."

If you want to completely take away the pain, hurt, and power someone or something has over you, forgiveness is the perfect solution. True forgiveness means you do not recognize any loss or pain. True forgiveness means completely letting go. True forgiveness makes the experience vanish. When the existence of past pain is removed, it can never bother you again.

If you're like me, then when someone's wronged you, you might've gone over the experience in your head and thought about what you should've said or what you should've done. I would even think about what I would say or do to them the next time I saw them.

Ultimately, what I was doing was re-creating the negative experience again and again. Even though I didn't have that same sense of shock as the first time around, my life still felt miserable when I focused on how I was wronged.

Looking at forgiveness as the sweetest form of revenge was the last piece of the puzzle needed for me to learn how to forgive. Forgiveness balanced the scales. I realized that true forgiveness gave me my freedom back. I was no longer plagued with thoughts of revenge, what I should have said or done. True forgiveness completely strips the offender of their power.

It is easy to write this and easy for you to read it, but we all still can make the practice of forgiveness tortuous. Why do we do this when we know that forgiving is our exit to freedom from resentment?

The answer is not to question why but to persist in practicing forgiveness. Just like persistence and gratitude, forgiveness is a skill that can only be perfected by use.

I challenge you further:

Accept your life as it is, and you will never have to blame anyone again. When you take responsibility for all the decisions you have made in your life, you will experience a freedom unlike anything else and open the pathways for joy and everything you've ever wanted to flow towards you.

By surrendering and accepting your life as it is now, the power of the past immediately dissolves and it's not impacting your future in the same way.

The truth is this: Your thinking, good or bad, has gotten you to this point in your life. Therefore, if you really want to be free, it is absolutely critical that you completely accept your life for what it is.

You cannot move forward to change your life for the better until you completely accept everything in your life for what it is.

Your attitude toward your job, house, spouse, car, friends, enemies, etc. are all the result of every thought and decision you have ever made. How much of that is made of resentment?

If you've been wondering why you keep having the same "stuff" and "problems," your answer is right here.

You keep holding on to the same resentments, your emotional baggage, and as you travel through life's vacation, you keep picking up more, weighing yourself down more and more until you finally collapse.

Get rid of your resentments.

1. Replace your resentments with gratitude.
2. Instead of allowing your resentments to have power over you, surrender to them, and learn from them.
3. Let your resentments be your instructors. Resentments can show you what you lack in life.
4. All your resentments lie in the past. By surrendering and accepting your life as it is, the past immediately has no power over you now or in your future. It is as simple as that.

You may find that you let a resentment go, and then one day out of the blue, you decide to go back, find it, and pick it up.

Picking resentment back up is insanity, right? Well, you're not totally crazy, because we've all done this. So, when you find yourself in that place again, ask yourself:

What benefit does having a resentment against this person, place or thing have for me? Is it helping me or is it hurting me?

Will this resentment get me what I want?

The process is the same whether it is a newly discovered resentment or one you have decided to pick up again. If you pick a resentment up again, simply accept that you have done it, and then ask yourself the same questions above, and observe.

Part of my story is a life full of resentment, blaming others for my position in life. I experienced two huge surges that moved me past this limitation. The first was the realization that I was fully responsible for my position in life. The second was the statement, "Forgiveness is the greatest revenge."

This statement made sense to me and immediately solved my need for revenge. True forgiveness is completely forgetting about it, a clean slate, it never happened. If it never happened, then there is no need for revenge, there is nothing to forgive.

If it never happened, then I have no reason to use my power of thought for anything other than the positive. Nothing will get a negative hold on me. Practicing true forgiveness, I do not forfeit the power of my thought over to someone else; I am not giving them anything to hold over me.

The truth is, I'm responsible, just like you're responsible. If you truly want to be free, it's critical you completely accept your life for what it is, because you can't move forward to change it for the better until you're able to accept responsibility for everything.

CHAPTER SUMMARY

Is resentment really a demonstration of what you lack in your life? Here is how I answered this question as a definite "YES" for myself.

When I asked myself if my resentment was a positive or negative in my life, the answer has been, is, and always will be negative. I then compared this to simple mathematics.

Addition and subtraction are opposite operations because one operation can "undo" the other. Adding 12 and 7 to get 19 is the opposite of 12 minus 7, leaving 5.

It made sense to me with this comparison that my feelings work in the same way with the quality of my life. Positive feelings added to more positive feelings create a higher number of positive experiences and feelings, where any negative feelings added in only subtract away from the total positive experience.

Resentment is a feeling that subtracts from the quality of life. Become more and more actively aware of your feelings, and arm yourself with feelings of gratitude. When you notice feelings of resentment, quickly rid yourself of them with gratitude so that they do not subtract from the total quality of your life.

As you practice this more and more, you will become acutely aware of the great danger resentment plays in your life, and you will become more prepared, ready, and able to once and for all completely let them go.

TRAINING EXERCISE

Most of us have plenty of examples in life where it is easy to see ourselves as the victim.

Take one negative experience and ask yourself if you are ready to quit giving total ownership to the people associated with this experience and claim it all yourself.

Look at this experience and ask yourself if you have been using it as an emotional crutch, leaning on it to explain away failure in your life.

Ask yourself if you can set it down now and walk away from it, just like you would baggage you no longer wish to carry. Think about what it would feel like to not be weighed down by this experience.

See yourself letting your emotional crutch go and walk away for good.

True forgiveness is returning the power back to yourself, rather than giving it over to someone.

Schedule time in your calendar daily for a forgiveness practice. Give yourself a notification reminder every day to do these exercises at the same time, if possible.

Use 'thought provokers,' objects that are visibly out of place, designed to make you stop and think about revisiting the practice of forgiveness.

GO DEEPER

This tool is one of the hardest for many people to use but is also the most powerful to completely get out of yourself. This tool will free you from the prison of resentment.

Instead of blaming someone else, choose differently. Choose to see the person who's hurt you as actually experiencing positivity.

This may be particularly hard for you, especially in the event you've been seriously wronged, as in when I was young and experienced sexual abuse.

Sometimes, this practice requires you speaking with a licensed professional or trusted advisor who can help you move through grief, wounding, and heartbreak — or even severe rage and resentment.

It's all okay. This is all your path towards enlightenment and becoming a more self-aware person.

Ask for forgiveness where you have been wrong. Keep your side of the street clean. Make amends where you have been wrong, but only in a way that does not bring any further harm to that person or someone else. Do not be selfish in asking for forgiveness.

It is easy to make a list of all the "SOBs" who have wronged you. Make that list, and then add your part to it.

What did that person do to you?

What did it have an effect on? Money? Pride? Relationships? Security? Self-esteem?

How did it make you feel?

Then the BIG question: What was your part in it? Were you to blame in any way?

113

If you were, do you owe an apology? If you do, consider the best way to do it. Consult the advice of a trusted friend or professional on the best way to approach asking for forgiveness if it is serious.

There is real power in admitting where you have made mistakes or need improvement. When you are able to be truly honest with yourself and others, you are able to be who you truly are and can grow and improve from there.

When you are hiding who you are, pretending to know or be someone you aren't, you limit yourself from growth.

What if your apology is not accepted? If you have made an honest attempt in making amends, there is nothing more you can do. You have swept your mess off of your side of the street. You have no power or right to control what they think or choose to hold on to. It is simply not your business. Do the next right thing and Think A Better Thought™. ⚘

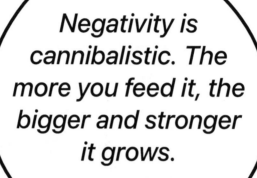

Negativity is cannibalistic. The more you feed it, the bigger and stronger it grows.

Bobby Darnell

CHAPTER 13
DELETE THE NEGATIVITY IN YOUR LIFE

Earlier in Chapter 10, I gave you an exercise where you were to try and focus simultaneously on both a negative and positive thought. This exercise proves that it is not possible for a negative and positive thought to be held in your mind together. Knowing this should motivate every person who wants to experience success in their life to actively monitor their thinking.

The more you can monitor your thoughts, the more you can optimize them and make sure they are positively charged, advancing you toward your goal. While this initial exercise only focused on two singular thoughts, I invite you to now consider expanding this technique to ALL your thoughts.

The ability to actively think, with focus and intention on creating your deepest desires is the hardest work on this earth. The hard work is not focusing our thoughts on what we desire; the hard work is keeping our focus. Removing thoughts of what we don't want when they enter our minds requires constant effort.

People who choose to work from the neck down, forfeiting their ability to actively think and create independently with their minds are mentally lazy. A mentally lazy person does not monitor thought and easily allows their thoughts to be negative. They procrastinate, blame people, places, and things for their problems; they choose to look at everything wrong in their life and what they lack.

Pointing your finger away from yourself is denial in its purest form. Right now, let's discover some truth together by observing our thoughts.

Ask yourself if you have blamed a person, place, or thing for a problem in your life recently.

Once you figure out who that person, place, or thing is (because we all do it), ask yourself if there is any benefit you are receiving by placing blame away from yourself.

Don't judge your answers. Observe them.

You can't try to be positive. You are either positive, or you are not. Positivity does not exist within any gray areas. It simply is or isn't.

Every positive experience adds to your life and every negative experience subtracts from your life. If you are constantly focused on what you do not have in a negative manner, how can you expect your situation to improve?

Negativity simply is a refusal to accept life as it is. And, the remedy for negativity is simple: replace a negative thought with a positive one!

Sure, it sounds easy, but like I mentioned earlier, the ability to actively think, with focus and intention on creating your deepest desires is the hardest work on this earth.

Sometimes negativity can be hiding in plain sight.

My marketing agency has enjoyed working with a variety of businesses, and from time to time we experience challenges not anticipated. A few years ago, we lost a client due to a simple misunderstanding. Here's the short story.

We were working on a tight schedule to complete a project. Roles with our client and my company were modified to help speed up production. Work from my company was completed and submitted for review right on schedule to the appropriate department. The problem is one of the employees of our client forgot that roles had been recently changed.

This person was no longer responsible for reviewing my company's work and became very irritated when the deadline arrived with nothing delivered to her. She sent one of my employees a series of emails and eventually a phone call that were not positive at all. This is a nice way to say it. The bottom line is that feelings were hurt at my company.

118

This person who worked for our client realized the mistake made, and made a very appropriate apology, and we all moved forward...I thought.

Unfortunately, after this experience, I made the mistake of letting our staff blow off steam by allowing a few jokes and comments to be made about this particular experience.

Initially, I thought it was positive for my staff to get over their feelings about what happened.

I could not have been more wrong.

The negative feelings grew, and we began to experience more problems with this account. Even though we never said anything negative directly to our client, they could absolutely feel the negative energy and vibration.

Within a few months of this initial misunderstanding, our client requested to end the relationship early, after only six months, which was a big blow.

I take 100% of the responsibility — I was wrong to allow our staff to communicate about our client in the way they did. While I absolutely encourage a safe communication zone, I now adhere to the rule that if you can't say something positive, you shouldn't say it at all.

Our old mentality was that we had a crappy client, but if that's what we thought, then why the heck would they want to stay working with us and investing in our services?

Instead of blaming our client we should have been asking questions like: "What can we do to prevent this in the future? How can we ensure that everyone working for our client feels valued and appreciated? What is the best possible outcome we could have from this experience?"

Negativity can only subtract. Take basic math for example: it is impossible for any number to grow by adding a negative.

The more negativity you allow in, the more positivity you're subtracting. ***Negativity will only take away from you and your growth.***

119

Thankfully, deleting negativity is pretty easy! All you have to do is replace the negative thought with a positive one.

What you did in Chapter 10 applies to every aspect of your life.

Your job is to recognize when you are thinking negatively and to immediately replace the negative thought with a positive one. The faster you can do this, the quicker you'll see results in your life.

Even if you forget to replace the negative thought until the next day, you are better off doing it then than unknowingly allowing the negative thought to continue on a destructive path inside your subconscious mind.

Be persistent in deleting the negativity in your life, and you will be surprised more and more with an abundance of great experiences.

CHAPTER SUMMARY

The more you can monitor your thoughts, the more you can optimize them and make sure they are positively charged, advancing you toward your goal.

The ability to actively think, with focus and intention on creating your deepest desires is the hardest work on this earth. The hard work is not focusing our thoughts on what we desire; the hard work is keeping our focus. Removing thoughts of what we don't want when they enter our minds requires constant effort.

Remember, a negative and positive thought cannot be held in your mind at the same time.

Random acts of kindness are excellent ways for you to act your way into better thinking.

Open a door for someone.
Let someone into your lane of traffic.

Smile when people look your way.
Put their grocery cart up for them.
Bring someone in your office a fresh cup of coffee.

There are thousands and thousands of possibilities all around you that don't cost a single penny where you can make a positive impact, even if it is small, on someone's life.

The more you start participating in serving and helping others, the faster you will rid yourself of negative experiences and thoughts.

TRAINING EXERCISE

It's time to turn your mistakes and failures into benefits.

Be grateful for them.

See them as instructors that have gotten you to where you need to go. Every mistake teaches you something, so be grateful that you're learning more with every mistake and even learn to adopt the attitude of looking forward to making more mistakes.

The more mistakes you make, the more you learn, leading you to greater and greater wins.

Write down three mistakes you regret making and then write down a positive experience that came as a result of each mistake.

_____

_____

_____

_____

Look at where you can be grateful for how these mistakes helped you grow.

_____

_____

_____

_____

GO DEEPER

Can you identify one of the biggest failures in your life? Do you still have thoughts where it feels like that past failure is still happening?

When we have major, negative experiences in our life there are very strong emotions associated. When they are not dealt with and corrected, we get "stuck," and the same "stuff" seems to keep happening over and over, like it is Groundhog Day.

The potential for your body to be addicted to negative emotions was discussed earlier. When we try to change, make progress, but then slip back to our old ways or state, this is a good indication of being addicted to a negative emotion.

It is even more probable when we keep the feelings of major negative experiences alive.

If you have a major failure that still has a negative effect on your emotions, ask yourself if it helps you or hurts you to beat yourself up about it.

Ask yourself if you were able to learn a valuable lesson.

Ask yourself if you would make the same mistake again knowing what you know now.

Ask yourself how you can turn this failure into a success.

When you have the emotional feelings of failure, combat them with thoughts of how you can turn that failure into a success. Even if all you are able to do is ask yourself, "How can I turn this failure into a success?", do that.

This simple shift in thinking about how to turn something into a benefit rather than wallowing in the misery of failure moves your thoughts and emotions to a positive state and sets you back on the right path.

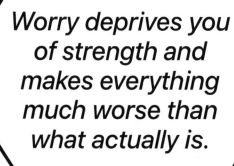

Worry deprives you of strength and makes everything much worse than what actually is.

Dr. Anil Kr Sinha

CHAPTER 14

THE WRECKAGE OF THE FUTURE

Right now, what are you worried about?

What problems do you have?

What people or circumstances do you believe are out to get you?

Think about them for a minute as we will come back to the answers of these three questions.

Let's break worry down for a second: what is worry really? Worry is a fear of a future event — in fact, it's the wreckage of the future.

Can you actually live in the future? Can you operate in the future? No.

You can only do what you are doing now in the present. Sure, you can plan ahead. When we plan ahead, we are doing it now, in the present moment.

Everything you do happens now. The time is always now.

I started my advertising agency in late December 2005. It was the second week of January 2006, and we did not have a single client. If we did not get a client soon, we would be out of business.

I remember coming up with the concept of fasting and making cold calls, hoping that God would have pity on us making this sacrifice of fasting and make us successful.

My wife went with me for support, and by 10:45 a.m., we possessed zero evidence of success. Not a single person was interested in our services. I stopped the car next to a city park. We prayed and cried about how hard it was, like we might never taste success again. What good did that do?

_, n., we were seated at my favorite Mexican restaurant enjoying a delicious lunch. So much for fasting.

We still did not have a client, but we did have enough to enjoy food, shelter, and many other conveniences. We were choosing to look at what was not real. The more we focused on what we didn't have, the more we created our own misery.

Worrying about not having any clients was almost driving us to the point of giving up. Yet, we persisted.

The next week, we made one sale. Then another. Then more. We were always given what we needed at every stage. And, upon reflection, we saw that even what we thought were monumental failures were actually stepping stones towards growth.

Now we know to look at each moment like the day we failed in fasting.

Think about it. We do not do anything in the future or the past. You experience everything in your life now. You have memories of past experiences and you are able to think about future experiences, but everything you have experienced in your life has always happened in the now.

Apply this concept of **NOW** to your problems. In all cases related to problems, the truth is that you are either dealing with a problem or you have accepted what happened.

There's no need to torture yourself over the future or the past. The past has already happened so the only choice really is to accept the past.

How much value does worry about future experiences really have for you?

The great Mark Twain said, "I am an old man and have known a great many troubles, but most of them never happened." I've had this same experience in my life.

Can you remember what you were worried about two weeks ago? Where is your worry now about those things? I've found that over a period of two weeks nearly everything I could worry about has magically been taken care of. Most of our worries never even happen.

Have you asked yourself these questions?

Right now, what are you worried about?

What problems do you have?

What people or circumstances do you believe are out to get you?

Think about all your previous worries. Did most of them happen, or were they as bad as you feared with your worry? When you were in the moment with those problems, what were you doing? You were dealing with them.

As bad as it may have been, you had everything you needed at that moment to deal with that problem. You have always had everything you need to deal with every problem you have ever had. This doesn't mean you dealt with all of them in the right way, but the truth is you've always been able to deal with problems when they needed to be dealt with.

You dealt with it. You accepted it and moved on. Did you worry about it after you dealt with it? Not if you had accepted it. Once you were there in the moment, dealing with the problem, there was no need or room for worry.

Recently I accompanied my wife to an appointment with a surgeon for a consultation. My wife has experienced many surgeries in her life. We have four children and having four human beings grow inside your body can take a toll.

Often, surgery has been the best or only solution for my wife. The day of this consultation she appeared anxious, even irritable at times. When I asked her why, she told me, "I'm nervous about everything the recovery is going to take — all the pain and discomfort."

She was very anxious, and I could feel her wanting to change her mind about the consultation.

"Are you experiencing pain right now?" I asked her.

"No," she responded.

"Will you be experiencing pain during the consultation?" I followed.

"No," she realized.

She hadn't even had the surgery, but in her mind, she was already there. She was completely overcome with fear.

"What's the benefit of worrying about pain right now? Is it helping you to worry?"

She thought about it for a moment.

"I know they haven't been fun, but haven't you been given everything you needed to make it through your previous surgeries?" I continued.

She thought a bit more, then replied definitively, "I have."

Once she fully embraced that worrying about a future outcome didn't have any benefit for her, the entire day became much more enjoyable. Things would be dealt with when they needed to be dealt with, but not in the now when they hadn't happened yet.

Here's what I mean about how worry wrecks the future.

We anticipate the worst-case scenario occurring.

We worry about future events.

The truth is the future is a time period in which we will never be living, because we can never live in the future — we can only live in the now.

128

You can pick a date and make plans, but those plans on that date will be occurring now. They will always be happening now. Now is all we have. Now is the only time period we are allowed to operate in, even though we can have memories of the past. Stay in the now and realize that you have always been given everything you need to take care of yourself now.

CHAPTER SUMMARY

Look at nature. Do you see animals or plants worrying? If animals could talk, what time would they tell you it is? They would say now. Time is simply a method created to measure experience.

We humans worry like it is a contest! We have actually made it "socially acceptable" to worry. Isn't that crazy? How easy is it to engage in a conversation about your problems?

Notice how you naturally feel like contributing to a friend's story of loss or sharing about a similar problem they are having the next time you are engaged in conversation with someone complaining. Notice how you want to "join the club of misfortune" and make your contributions of failure and loss. Your worries literally create what you worry about.

Observe when you worry about problems. Ask yourself if there is any benefit to you worrying about it. Ask yourself if worry will fix the problem. If you are going to have to deal with your problems anyway, what is the benefit of worrying about them? Simply observe your answers. Observe them and do nothing else. You will see your worries drift away as if by magic.

What is the point of worrying then? Ask yourself, "What benefit does worrying give me?" Can you find any benefit? Really search. Dig deep. We all have been picking up worries our entire lives. There has to be some benefit to worrying then, right, especially if we all do it?

The truth is that there really is no benefit to worrying. If there is no benefit, then why do we constantly make the choice to worry? It is time for you to delete worry entirely.

TRAINING EXERCISE

Let's take a moment to really hone the answer to this question:

What's the point of worrying?

Ask yourself, "What benefit does worrying give me?"

Can you truly find a positive benefit?

I want you to really search. I want you to dig deep. I want you to think about all the worries you've had your entire life and see if there really is a big benefit.

Why do we constantly CHOOSE to worry?

Yep, that's right, I said, "choose."

In every moment, you have a choice.

You have the free will to choose what will or won't serve you.

And, if you take a look at the example Mother Nature has offered to us, then you might see animals and plants don't spend their time worrying, because they're constantly focused on the present moment.

Knowing that in every present moment, you're okay, then what have you got to worry about?

I've noticed that it's become socially acceptable to worry...it's easy to engage in a conversation about your problems, rather than your successes.

The next time you're engaged with someone who's complaining, ask yourself if you want to join this club of misfortune, or if you could choose to talk about something positive.

GO DEEPER

Poise is the opposite of worry. Acting with poise is acting within a state of balance. Someone with poise possesses steadiness, composure, and demonstrates ability, living in a dignified, self-confident manner.

Poise is completely demonstrated when you know what you want, and you also know how to do it. Take driving for example. An experienced driver has poise. There is no thinking about driving that needs to be done. Every move, checking the rear-view mirror, turning on blinkers, changing lanes, coming to a stop, driving the appropriate speed, watching out for obstructions and dangers, etc. are all automatic.

I demonstrate poise as a driver today, but I did not when I was learning how to drive. There were plenty of times where I easily demonstrated worry to myself and everyone around me. But, as I practiced the action of driving and learned from my mistakes, I became more and more confident with my driving to where now, today, I drive with poise.

Notice, I mention the "action" of driving, not the "thinking" of driving. If thinking was enough, I would have had everything I needed to drive by watching the videos and reading instructions in my drivers' education class. You can have the thought to be a poised driver, but only action by driving will give you the opportunity to really be a poised driver.

Whether you have poise or not today does not matter. What matters is this: Do you want poise in every move you make? If you do, then you have to start ACTING WITH POISE.

Keep at it. If you make a mistake, learn from it and do not make the same, exact mistake again. Every mistake has an equivalent opportunity for success.

When every move you make is intended to be full of poise, you are unstoppable. Even when you make a mistake you are still successful, because you are learning how to constantly have poise in your life.

131

A mistake only means you figured out a way not to do things. All that is left at that point is to not do that same thing the same way again.

Turn your worry into poise. ⚱

To accomplish the perfect perfection, a little imperfection helps.

Dejan Stojanovic

CHAPTER 15

WHAT'S WRONG WITH PERFECTION?

You may believe a baby is born perfect. Whether that is true or not, the fact is that if a baby is born perfect, he or she does not stay perfect for very long. A baby learns by making mistake, after mistake, after mistake - and thank goodness they never give up.

The first thing you notice with a baby is that it really does nothing but cry, eat and poop. Then one day you notice that they wake up a bit and start observing the environment around them. They are soaking up everything like a sponge.

There is no judgment from the baby, because how could a baby judge anything, right? They start to move, try to sit up, fall over, make noises with their mouth, and try to talk, slobbering all over their face and clothes. They crawl and fall. They try to walk and fall, many times scraping or bumping, causing a good cry. Are they crying because they are hurt or frustrated? Could be both, right? But they don't quit.

And then one day, out of the blue, they walk. Soon after, they're running. They say their first word. Almost just as quickly, they're talking in sentences.

What would happen to the human race if one day babies started worrying about making mistakes? What if they became so worried about making a mistake, that they thought it would be safer just to stay where they are and cry, eat, poop, and nothing else?

What if babies worried about what their parents and other people around them thought about their mistakes? What if they just decided it would be safer not to even try? Our race would be in big trouble then, wouldn't it?

Mistakes and failures are our best way to learn. The natural system of learning is to "fail forward." It is what we are given to start out life with. Who are we to come up with a better plan for learning than nature?

135

Turn your mistakes and failures into benefits. Be grateful for them. See them as stepping stones that are helping you attain your ultimate desire. Know that every mistake is teaching you how to attain your greatest desire and be grateful that you are learning more with every mistake.

If you're having thoughts where you're beating yourself up, then it's time to take a look at your ego again. Remember, your ego knows everything about you, and it knows exactly how to attack your weakest points. Your ego is rooted in the past and will create false thinking.

Who is the easiest person for you to attack? You. It is easy to get caught up with seeing everything wrong about yourself.

Every day, all around you, advertising messages constantly promote pills, programs, and products that will "fix" your problems. We look at the successes of celebrities and the rich, and envy their position in life.

We try weight loss programs and get rich quick schemes, hoping for an easy, quick solution to our problems. The truth is none of these quick fixes work. There might be a short-term improvement, but we usually wind up right back where we started.

The reason is we aren't addressing the real problem, which is we are unhappy inside. We fail to improve our internal condition because we constantly seek the answers to our problems outside ourselves.

Science tells us that there is no identical leaf on any tree alive. Science also tells us that there is not a single, identical snowflake. You are just as unique.

You are the only one of you that will ever be. You were born with a combination of unique attributes, physical and mental, that no one else has. Your perceptions and ideas are like no one else's.

Rare-jewels, works of art, and landmarks are considered priceless and irreplaceable because they are the only ones on earth. Guess what?

You are the only you on this earth and also, are priceless. You are a masterpiece that will never be duplicated.

Sticks and Stones May Break My Bones, But Words Will Never Hurt Me

It's rare that I ever meet anyone who doesn't feel a compelling need to be liked by others. It's part of our DNA, this desire to belong or to be part of a tribe, both from a purely physical perspective and a mental-emotional one as well.

Ask yourself this question: "Does what other people think about me help me in any way? Does it hurt me?"

When my family and I went to Iceland, it was the first time that we bonded together without giving a care to what anyone else thought.

Even though my kids were 15, 16, 19, and 21 at the time, and in that tender, teenager space...where everything anyone thinks about them matters tremendously...they let themselves be absolute oddballs and goofballs, because they realized that they didn't know anyone on the trip, nor would anyone ever follow up with them about anything.

My teens could be free not to worry about what ANYONE thought and simply enjoy one another's company, as well as the experience of being in this beautiful country abroad.

Your thoughts – not anyone else's – are what you have control over. You have no control over what others think. Furthermore, you have no access at all to what is going on with their thought processes. If you think you know what they think about you, you're indulging in the worst kind of fictionalizing.

Most of us wind up wasting tons of time and energy trying to influence what other people think about us. Yet, these people either disappoint us because they can never live up to our expectation of what they should think about us, or we agonize, because we are clueless about what they actually think about us. How could there be any other outcome?

Do you think it is possible that most of the population experiences the same challenges, where their egos are running their shows? If this is possible, do you really think they even have a real opinion of you?

When playing the comparison and people-pleasing game, we can find ourselves up against a wall that either we're inevitably disappointing someone else or they're unable to live up to our expectations.

Individually, we create the law of our lives by seeing what we choose to see.

If we choose to see ugliness, envy, hate, sorrow, lust, poverty and want, then that is what we will experience in our lives. If we choose to see happiness, abundance, love, fun and excitement, then we will experience these things.

Thoughts are real things. Your thoughts create your reality.

Accept and embrace your life as it is. Accept that others have opinions about you which you have no control over. Accept that it is not your business what someone else thinks, especially about you. Accept that you do not have to be perceived as perfect by others.

This is important. People, places, and things have no power over you. Until you truly know this, you are limiting your experience. Let's dig in a little further.

Accept that others opinion of you is their business and not yours, freeing you from worrying about their opinion. Accept that you and only you can make sure you think what you want to think.

What you think is really the only thing that matters because what you think will determine who you are and what you have. When you start to wonder about what other people think about you, immediately stop and instead visualize something positive in their life happening for them.

Visualize them enjoying family, a vacation, or a nice evening out. Switch the focus of your thought from worrying about their opinions to something beneficial for them, and your worry will fade away.

Just think about how freeing this can be! At the end of the day, the opinions of others hold zero value for you, because you have absolutely no control over what anyone else thinks about you. And, what anyone else thinks about you is none of your business!

CHAPTER SUMMARY

Ask yourself, "Do the opinions of others have any benefit for me?" Observe the answer. If you are telling yourself, "yes," then that is your ego talking. The opinions of others hold zero value to you.

Does someone else's judgment of you have any real value for you? Does their judgment make up who you are? If you think it does, what makes you think it does? How is it this way? Who gives this person permission to shape who you are with their judgment of you?

This person is you. Take back ownership of your life. The only person who can give permission to shape who you are is you. You have 100 % full control over who you are. Use this thought control intelligently. Does knowing this mean that you will not be judged? No. Knowing you have complete control of your thought means that you can focus your thought on the truth of who you are.

TRAINING EXERCISE

If you're not feeling okay with being imperfect and find that you're beating yourself up with thoughts you'd never say to a friend, then ask yourself this:

Can I absolutely prove this belief without a shadow of a doubt?

If you can't, then it's not true.

That simple question right there can begin to open the pathway for you to garner more compassion for yourself and all the ways you're learning as you grow.

Keep a beginner's mind, always learning, where you never take anything for granted and always revisit the grandest of life's lessons from an open perspective.

The more energy we spend trying to make someone else like us, the less attention we have on honoring ourselves in the ways that'll make us most joyful.

You have 100% full control over who you are.

You can choose whether you allow someone else to judge you in a way that impacts your own well-being.

Can you accept that others will have an opinion of you, no matter what?

Can you visualize something positive happening in your own life? Then, think about something beneficial happening for someone else?

Can you continue to cultivate this feeling of goodness, so that everyone wins?

Accept that you have 100% full control over who you are and take charge!

GO DEEPER

Has your quest for perfection programmed your subconscious mind with thoughts of failure and defeat? Can you think back to a time in life where you missed hitting a goal and what your thoughts were?

Think about all the times you have mentally beat yourself up, and ask yourself if what you were thinking about you would be the same words you would use with a friend.

I learned that my subconscious was full of negative thoughts about myself. These thoughts were input over many different experiences I perceived to be negative.

I also learned that the only way for me to get rid of these negative, personal thoughts was to flood them out with positive, true thoughts about myself.

And I also learned that only through the practice of consistent daily positive, personal affirmations of at least one month could the negative thoughts be flushed out.

I took my favorite personal affirmations from my favorite books and recorded audio files to play back to myself. You can do this with any smart phone, and even add some relaxing background music.

I listen to my affirmations every morning upon waking, various times though the day, and before going to bed. I always feel better, more relaxed, and confident when listening to them. You will too if you will take the time to find, write, and record them.

Here is one of my favorites from the audio book, *The Science of Getting Rich,* "I can succeed. All that is possible to anyone is possible to me. I am successful. I do succeed for the power of success is full inside me. This is the simple truth."

Create one or more positive affirmations to read aloud daily. If you are wondering how to come up with a positive affirmation, just Google "positive affirmations." Hundreds of websites and resources are available for free to get you started.

I have written, revised, deleted, resurrected, and re-written affirmations for over twenty years. There is one thing I have learned, they never stop evolving. As I change, my affirmations change.

There is always something new and exciting to work toward.

141

If you want to take it even further and have a very long list of affirmations, you can record them and play them back to yourself. This has been proven to be one of the very best methods of reaching your subconscious mind before going to bed.

I highly encourage you to start by setting aside five minutes a day at the same time. Keep it consistent and remain persistent about doing them.

You will need at least 30 consecutive days of reading the same affirmation for it to start to take effect. Remember the NASA goggles study I mentioned at the beginning of the book? ⚚

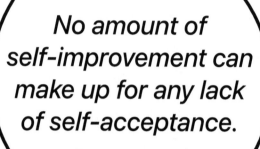

No amount of self-improvement can make up for any lack of self-acceptance.

Robert Holden

CHAPTER 16

STOP HATING YOURSELF

You're stupid.
You're ignorant.
You're lazy.
You're afraid.

How often do you hear statements like that inside your head?

Take a few minutes and be totally honest with yourself.

We have already covered not worrying about what others think. You are completely safe here to observe the truth.

Who is coming up with these "beliefs" above? Your ego, of course.

Your ego knows you better than anyone else. You have to give your ego some credit. The ego is marvelously talented at tricking us into many things we do not want, including thinking much less of ourselves.

How do we allow this to keep happening over and over?

Ask yourself what benefits you receive by calling yourself stupid, ignorant, lazy or weak.

Ask yourself this question slowly.

Your ego is going to try to distract you from observing the answer.

Did you feel a little different after you asked yourself those questions? I know I did, and I was amazed that I had allowed this pattern of beating myself up to go on for so long unnoticed. No one but me was doing this. I was 100 % responsible for telling myself I was those things.

Did I come up with them on my own? No, these thought patterns of self-abuse were learned over time by my experiences with others. I've directly been called stupid and ignorant before. This is an easy insult for anybody to use toward another person, and somewhere during my journey my ego picked these insults up to use against me, too.

I take full responsibility now.

Before, my ego would pull the weapon of choice out of its arsenal, effectively using it against me. I still catch this happening today, but now I know what's going on, and I can immediately stop it if I choose to.

Why would I choose not to? An intelligent person would say, you should always choose to stop your ego from using its weapons against you.

My ego still beats me from time to time.

Here are a few things I have learned about my ego.

My ego makes absolutely no sense. It operates in a state of fear of change. My ego bases all evidence on past experiences, and it uses those experiences to keep me from advancing.

When you let your guard down, your ego goes into attack mode. How do you observe your ego? Ask yourself questions.

Here are a few you should ask yourself often:

> What am I thinking about?

> Why am I thinking this?

> Is what I'm thinking going to help me or hurt me in getting what I want?

> Who is speaking, my ego or my consciousness?

146

Your ego cannot hide from observation. When you feel your thoughts spiraling out of control, then it's time to stop and ask yourself these or similar questions to regain control.

When I was a kid, I'd go to my grandmother's house after school where *Looney Tunes*, *The Brady Bunch*, and *Gilligan's Island* were the regular after school TV programming. Short commercials would play in between the cartoons, usually every day, featuring a little character floating through a human body singing a song that shared the message: "You are what you eat from your head down to your feet."

Hard to argue against this, right? If you stuff your face with $30 worth of fast food every day, there's a good chance that you'll be overweight, develop heart disease, diabetes, and eventually die many years before you should.

If I were to remake that commercial now, I'd share this message:

You are what you think you are.

In my experience, there's a lot of hate towards successful people, where comments like: "They think they are so special. They sure are proud of themselves. He just thinks he is better than everyone else," run on repeat.

Given all that I've shared so far, what thoughts do you think successful people actually have about themselves?

They don't care what other people think or say, and instead, have positive, enriching thoughts about themselves and everyone else. They claim greatness and embrace having more.

Even amidst doubt, they find the path that builds confidence and poise. They think success. They think abundance. They think prosperity. They think health. They think wealth. They think happiness.

They do not waste their thought on lack, poverty, sickness, or want. They live in a state of gratitude.

You are what you think you are. Start thinking abundance, life, happiness, health, wealth, prosperity, excitement, adventure, and gratitude. Think what you want to experience and be.

Look at your life right now. Look at the relationships you have, your career, family, health. Are you completely satisfied with all aspects of your life? If not, then what areas do you want to change? Write them down.

Now review what thoughts you have about these areas you want to change. Are you thinking thoughts that are exactly what you do not want? Look at all the thoughts, the ones you are conscious of and the ones that come out of nowhere.

Keep in mind this fact: Where your attention goes, energy flows. In other words, if you are focusing your attention on people, places, and things you do not want in your life, it is going to be very hard for you to get rid of them because you are giving ample attention to them with your thought.

If you're having trouble reviewing what you've been thinking, go through your social media posts. Read what you have been broadcasting to the world.

For some of my Facebook friends, very little seems to go right in their lives. There is always drama with someone offending them, something breaking, or some other unique conflict.

Not only are these people thinking negatively a high percentage of the time, but they also have all their friends fueling their negativity with more negative thoughts about how bad their life must really be.

These people constantly post about what is wrong in their lives and invite others to join in commenting on their personal misery, and guess what? More wrong always shows up because they are broadcasting to everyone that they prefer to think about and operate in conflict and drama.

What are you broadcasting to the world about yourself? Every thought you have is a real thing, a real creation. Think of your body and mind like a TV or radio station, broadcasting your personal channel for the Universe to tune in.

148

Each thought is an advertisement, an invitation, to the world. Like-minded people, places, and things on similar thought frequencies are going to tune in and respond to your invitation. If you do not like what is showing up in your life, then you need to change the thoughts you are broadcasting.

Remember a positive and negative thought about you cannot exist at the same time.

By breaking the habit and pattern of thinking badly about yourself, and replacing bad thinking with positive thinking about yourself, this simple solution can profoundly change your life!

CHAPTER SUMMARY

My ego does know me better than anyone else, so I should expect it to patiently wait to attack, especially when I become used to it not showing up. I should also expect my ego to go after my weaknesses.

Does an enemy attack another enemy's strength? No, the enemy attacks your weakest point where the most harm can be made. The ego operates in the same manner. I am very good about keeping my guard up, but I have learned that I can get too comfortable in my confidence.

I can believe I have beaten my ego and that it is not going to show up again. When this happens, I usually have a slip where my ego will dominate. It is very frustrating, and it used to cost me several days of progress. Today, I can stop it before it happens by monitoring my feelings, and you can too.

The practice of monitoring your thought makes perfect sense when you consider what other vital statistics we monitor on a regular basis. Our blood pressure, blood sugar, weight, heart rate, calories, and many other vital statistics are often checked.

Why do we check them? It gives an accurate report of where our health is, right? It allows us or doctors to be preemptive in treating or preventing illness or disease. It makes even more sense for us to do this with our thought because nothing happens without a thought first.

┌─ TRAINING EXERCISE ─────

Write down and memorize three positive thoughts about yourself.

Practice using each thought at random times throughout the day.
Place thought provokers around your home and work environments
to prompt you re-enforcing a positive thought about yourself.

GO DEEPER

Check your emotional vitals. Before going to sleep each night review your
day. Were you present in all your thinking, or did you allow your ego to take
control?

Realize when you were successful in staying present.

Realize when your ego took control and ask yourself what you can do to
prevent that same, negative result in the future.

What were you feeling? What were you doing? Know the answers so that
you don't put yourself in the same position again. Make a decision to have a
different outcome and visualize that happening before going to sleep.⅄

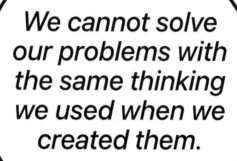

We cannot solve our problems with the same thinking we used when we created them.

Albert Einstein

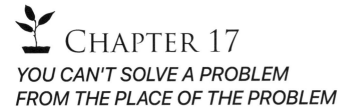

CHAPTER 17

YOU CAN'T SOLVE A PROBLEM FROM THE PLACE OF THE PROBLEM

Do you easily fall asleep? Do you wake up excited to experience a new day? For years, I did not.

I would lie in bed, nearly falling asleep, and then suddenly wake up with what seemed to be thousands of thoughts populating in my mind. I would think of work that needed to be done, mistakes that had been made, mistakes that might be made, and people who had wronged me, on and on.

I don't know how I would fall asleep, but it would take a while, sometimes hours, only for me to wake up, immediately being bombarded with all the problems I was going to have to deal with that day.

It was such a terrible way to live. The good news is that this pattern of going to sleep and waking up with problems can be solved within a few days. The bad news is that it is so simple to solve that most people miss it completely. They are so trained with entertaining their "problems" that they give nearly zero effort in solving them.

You can't solve a problem from the place of the problem — you have to come at it from the place of the solution.

Where your attention goes, energy flows. This is the Law of Attraction. The energy and vibration of what you are thinking and feeling is what's attracting similar energy and experiences into your life. So, rather than focusing on your worries or your problems, a better option is to focus on what your desired outcome is.

What is a honey bee attracted to? Most people would simply say, "a flower," but the honey bee only visits a blossomed flower, not one with a tightly closed bud. The blossomed flower is the only one providing any

153

benefit to the bee because the bee cannot gather pollen and nectar from a closed bud.

The bee is not the only one who benefits. The flower is advanced by the bee becoming a pollinator with other flowers, which is required for the flowers to reproduce and advance.

Think of yourself as a flower. If you are tight and closed up, you are less likely to attract the people, places, and things in your life to help you get what you most desire. You have to open up. Open your thinking and feelings, allow your mind to be open, not closed.

When we hold our focus on our problems from a negative perspective and not a solution, we close up. Closing up makes it much harder to solve the problem.

In Chapter 7, you were given a tool to zone out, relax, and recharge. This is one of my favorite tools to solve problems because it requires the least amount of effort in helping me open up to a solution.

Here is exactly how I do it:

I lie down on my couch, and I say out loud, "Solve this problem."

I then go through the practice outlined in Chapter 7 of raising and then letting fall my arms and legs. I then say, "Solve this problem," out loud again, and I think about the feeling and experience of solving that problem.

I don't worry about the amount of time I am relaxing; I just relax until I feel like getting back up from my couch. My average time is twenty minutes.

There have been days when finishing this exercise that I immediately have the answer to my problem, but most of the time the answer comes later. I don't worry about having the answer. I stay grateful in knowing I will receive it from whatever source when the time is right.

Today, I know I will receive it because I have practiced this exact exercise time after time without failing.

Find the tools that work best for you to stay solution focused by using them on your problems today. Take action. You won't know which tools are best unless you use them.

CHAPTER SUMMARY

By focusing your thoughts on gratitude, the solution, and your desired outcome, rather than how bad the problem is, you're opening yourself up to receiving the solution.

Take a short break from this book to watch a YouTube video from the NASA Jet Propulsion Laboratory. Here is the link: https://www.thinkabetterthought.com/pixel/

If you didn't watch the video, what you would have seen is this:

On February 14, 1990, Voyager 1 took a picture a distance of 3.7 billion miles from the Earth. This image is known as the "Pale Blue Dot."

The Earth appears in the picture as a single pixel object.

How big do you really think you are now? How big do you think your mistakes are? How big are your failures?

This planet that we live on shows up as a single pixel in a photograph from space in 1990.

A single pixel.

Think of all that happens on this earth and the power of Mother Nature. Think of how big it all seems. Consider the size of your problems when our planet is reduced to a single pixel on a photograph. Consider this photo was taken from our solar system. We are but a speck of dust in the universe.

TRAINING EXERCISE

Where are you putting most of your energy? On the problem or on the solution?

Can you allow yourself to dream about the ideal outcomes?

Do you feel worthy of receiving all the goodness and abundance the Universe wants to bestow upon you?

Turn your mistakes and failures into benefits.

Be grateful for them.

See them as instructors that have gotten you to where you need to go. Every mistake teaches you something, so be grateful that you're learning more with every mistake and even learn to adopt the attitude of looking forward to making more mistakes.

The more mistakes you make, the more successes you have, leading you to greater and greater wins.

See yourself making more and more successes all the time.

When you've had an experience that you didn't like the outcome of, revise the memory in your thought before going to bed.

You can create any experience in your mind, and you have the absolute right to re-create any previous memory. Use this with your problems.

Turn your thinking away from focusing on the problem and create a memory of experiencing the benefits of the solution. Focus on the benefits and not how the problem was solved.

GO DEEPER

Come from the solution.

What eliminates a problem? A solution.

You need to come from the place of the solution, rather than the place of the problem, if you really want things to be different.

1. Focus only on solving one problem at a time.
2. Quit trying to solve your problems from the neck down.

Take these two examples:

Before Bed

I'm lying in bed at the end of the day, ready for sleep. I have a problem, and that problem is I need to hire a quality sales person. I have interviewed several people, but there is not a quality candidate.

I can lie in bed and worry about how there are no quality candidates. I can think about the time I have wasted meeting with unqualified people. I can think that I will not be able to find a solution. I can think about every other company but mine being able to easily hire sales people.

Is this thinking true? I am certainly making it true in my mind by letting this negative thinking continue to be created. This kind of thinking has a very good chance of preventing me from getting the rest I desire. It has a profoundly negative effect on the chance of even a decent night's sleep.

A better option is to focus my thought before going to sleep on my desired outcome. Instead of thinking about what I do not have, I daydream before falling off to sleep, visualizing the perfect sales person enjoying success with my company.

I have a much better chance of resting, and I have an even better chance of waking up to a solution because my subconscious mind has had the entire

157

night to work toward an answer instead of working on what I do not desire, my problem.

Waking Up

The waking up example uses the same problem of needing to hire a quality sales person.

I awake in dread. I have an even more intense recitation of my problem than while I was laboring to go to sleep; because, now it is morning. What I dread is about to happen. I fully expect that I will receive a dismal experience with each interview.

Or, those first moments upon awakening where I may lie in bed and doze for a bit is an excellent opportunity for me to say to myself, "Solve the sales person problem," and then fall back to sleep for a few moments.

This is another opportunity for me to hand the problem off to my subconscious mind, instead of letting the problem of not having a quality sales person linger in my conscious thought.

Focusing my thought on the solution, the desired outcome, and not the problem allows me to be much more receptive to a solution. If I am spending my thought and energy on the problem, I am more likely to be closed to receiving the solution.

Keeping a clean mind, free of infection from negative thought is a lifelong duty, along with persistence, if you desire success. Something as simple as a small problem can be turned into a furious rage of negative thinking, separating you from the path to success. What you think before going to bed and upon awakening are monumental influencers on the environment you live in. ⚘

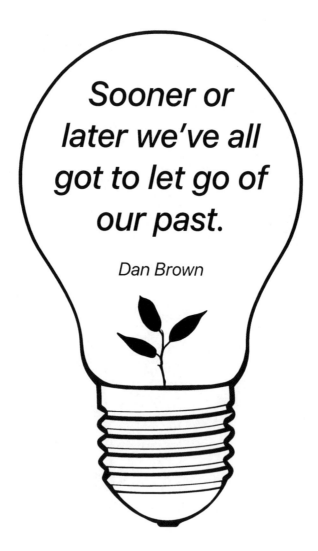

Sooner or later we've all got to let go of our past.

Dan Brown

CHAPTER 18

LET GO OF THE VICE GRIP ON PAIN

Everyone suffers pain. No one's immune to it. Whether it's physical, mental, or even spiritual, we all feel pain.

It's not right for us to judge someone else's pain, because we'll never have the same exact experience they did. We'll never have the exact same perspective as anyone else, either.

Carrying pain is a conscious choice and even though someone else may be the initial cause of our suffering, we're responsible for whether or not it continues to live on within us.

Regardless of what kind of pain we have, there's one element we share in common: we can choose how much we want to hold onto our hurts.

Holding on to pain carries nearly as much negative power as resentment.

During my senior year of high school, I was cut from the varsity baseball team.

As I walked up to the locker room and read the list of players who had made the team, I scanned up and down the list, but my name wasn't there.

"This has got to be a mistake," I thought to myself.

Four freshman players had made the team, and here I was, a senior, but I hadn't made the cut. Being sure that this was a mistake, I went to the coach.

"Shane," he said to me, looking me square in the eyes, "you just weren't hitting the ball well."

I didn't agree! I felt I had been crushing the ball as well or better than anyone else. But it was his choice to make for me to be on the team or not, and he had made his decision.

The resentment that I harbored for this man accumulated throughout the rest of my high school career — and beyond. I was filled with thoughts of hate for the man. I wanted him to experience pain and humiliation.

For the next 20 years, I kept re-living the feelings of being cut over and over again a few times a year.

I even blamed this experience for mistakes I'd make later down the line as an adult. As much as I tried to let it go, I also relished it.

By assaulting this man in my thoughts, I had an excuse for not having what I wanted. This memory and method became an emotional crutch I could use at any time to explain away failure to myself.

Before the dinner party of my 20-year high school reunion, I drove past the baseball field and noticed it had been named after that same coach.

"Well, I guess he must have died," I said to my wife.

The thought of his death made me feel a little better.

I was still alive, and he wasn't.

Later that night, when we entered the party, I was surprised to see my old football coach, who I had a tremendous amount of respect for. He had been invited by the reunion committee and had accepted.

It was great to see him, but standing right next to him was the baseball coach who had cut me from the team, still alive. "Unbelievable," was the word that I heard myself saying inside my mind.

There were two men in their late 70s standing, greeting former students. The one on the left I held great respect for. The one standing on the right I considered punching in the throat. I confidently walked up and shook my

162

football coach's hand.

He barely remembered me, and my former baseball coach had no idea who I was.

What I had carried for 20 years instantly became meaningless. I was continually choosing to relive this painful moment on my own. In fact, I was the only person in the world who even remembered it!

Out of a graduating class of 373, only 30 showed up to the reunion, and not one person knew what I had been a slave to for 20 years.

Carrying pain is not an accident; it's a conscious choice, and we make that choice on our own.

How do you put your pain down? Just put it down.

Say to yourself, "I am no longer going to carry this pain with me," or a similar sentence in your own words.

Visualize yourself putting it down, just like the suitcases full of resentments we dropped in Chapter 12. If you pick the pain up later, whether it is a minute, hour, day or week, go through the exercise of putting it down again. You are the only one who can carry your pain. Put it down. Drop it!

See yourself letting the pain go and existing without it. Remember you do not have to be perfect at anything except not giving up. PERSIST in letting go of your pain.

CHAPTER SUMMARY

The more you resist hurt, the more it hurts.

The more you blame someone else, the more you feel like the victim.

The more you aren't able to forgive, the more you're stuck in the vice grip of pain.

Give yourself the grace of letting go.

─ TRAINING EXERCISE ─

Go back to the example earlier in the book where each resentment or pain you hold on to is like a suitcase you are responsible for keeping up with everywhere on your journey through life.

How heavy is this suitcase you are carrying? Can you imagine enjoying your journey more without having to drag it around everywhere with you?

Think of the very essence of your resentment or pain. Find where you hurt the most with it.

Now ask yourself what the opposite of this pain is. Ask yourself questions like:

> How can I turn this pain or resentment into a benefit to me?
>
> What can I learn from this pain?
>
> How can I be grateful for the experience of this pain?

Do not worry if you do not receive the answer right away. If you do not, schedule a time every day to ask yourself the same question(s) until you do receive an answer.

GO DEEPER

Once you do receive the answers to turning your resentment or pain into a benefit, focus on it. Remind yourself to come back to this answer and focus on it whenever your resentment or pain pops up.

You may need to practice your gratitude for it several times before the pain or resentment starts to fade away.

Remember, where your attention goes energy flows. By focusing your thought away from resentment and pain, you are taking energy away and starving your pain.

Practice this with persistence and soon you will no longer know the pain you have been carrying all through life. ⚱

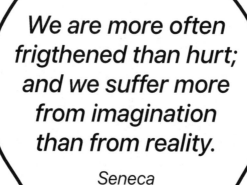

We are more often frigthened than hurt; and we suffer more from imagination than from reality.

Seneca

 # CHAPTER 19

MASTERING FEAR AND TEARING DOWN THE WALLS

Fear is an extremely negative emotion caused by a belief that someone or something is dangerous and likely to cause harm or a threat.

Fear, anxiety, and depression are our own creation. It is easier to be afraid than it is to consciously think. This is why so many of us stay trapped by fear. We don't actively try to conquer it.

The more you know about how destructive fear is, the more you know how to overcome the aspects of your life that are holding you back.

I want you to take a look back at the skills you have been learning and developing up to this point:

Persistence

Knowing your ego

Monitoring your feelings

Relaxing and recharging

Recognizing success in your life

Living with gratitude 24/7

Removing all resentments

Practicing forgiveness

Deleting negativity

Removing worry

Not needing to be perfect

Not worrying about what others think

Deleting self-hatred

Living solution focused

Letting pain go

You should feel very good about the progress you have made. Take a moment to be grateful, to thank yourself for being honest and doing the work. Take a moment to feel great about learning how to use your new set of skills.

These skills are needed to tear down the walls that you have built around you with fear, keeping pain in and good out. I built walls as high as mountains around me. If I was exposed to pain, a wall went up to try and keep a similar experience from happening again, but the walls kept all the pain inside me.

Have you ever seen the outside of a prison? What surrounds it? An inescapable wall or fence, right? When I was able to ask myself the right questions and observe the answers, I was able to see that I had been living in a self-constructed prison of fear.

Ask yourself if you have any walls built around you for protection. Ask if they are keeping pain out, or if they are holding you as a prisoner of pain and fear.

We were not designed by Creation to be isolated. We were designed to be cooperative with each other, working together to advance Creation. We were designed to recognize and work with the Living Creation inside of us.

You have to tear down all walls you have built around you because these walls are keeping the most important partner in your life outside, unable to help you.

It's time to talk about What makes everything work together. It's time to bring in the Ultimate Partner for Success, God.

The words "God" or "spiritual" might put you off. They both did for me many times over a 30-year period.

So, if you are saying to yourself, "Oh god, not God!" I understand how you feel.

Before going further, I want to make it clear that I believe your faith is your business. I am not promoting any religion or telling you what you need or have to believe.

I am sharing the experience of recreating the conception of my Higher Power, who I choose to call God. I discovered through the use of the exercises and tools I have given to you that my relationship with God was destructive and had to be changed for me to realize happiness.

Many religions teach not to question your beliefs, that questioning your faith is blasphemy, but I could not disagree more. You have the right to ask any question.

Knowing this today gives me the green light to question every belief I have. And, the more I can remind myself that TRUTH will always survive any observation, the more I can use this method flawlessly to reevaluate the beliefs in my life.

There was a point in my 30s where I completely turned my back on God.

"I won't ask You for anything, and You leave me alone." This was the extent of my relationship with God. I didn't want God in my life. I was afraid if I asked God for anything, it would come at a price I was not willing to pay.

I blamed God for everything, and I developed a deep resentment towards God.

The last thing I wanted to do at this point in my 30s was talk or hear about God. "I've had enough of God," is what I would tell you, or "No thanks." So, if you have had or have similar feelings when you hear "God," it's ok. It's not where you start; it's where you finish that matters.

All Truth survives observation, and if you truly observe what you believe with persistence, there is no question that you will discover your Truth.

For two years in a row, I had perfect attendance in Sunday school at my local church. I was "saved" many times. However, I bought the idea that if I broke God's rules, I'd be in real trouble, so the more rules I broke, the more it made sense for me to separate myself from God. I didn't want any trouble from Him.

Before long, I felt like I didn't have any hope at all.

"Why bother," I thought to myself. "I've already ruined everything."

Separating myself from God, from a source of unconditional love, was nothing but a choice to separate myself from everything good. This does not mean that I did not have good things in my life during this period, or that I completely ignored God and my relationship with Him. I just blocked God from having any real impact on my life.

Let's take a moment to observe your current environment.

> This book you are reading or listening to.
>
> The chair you are sitting in or the ground you are standing on.
>
> The air you are breathing.
>
> Your clothes.
>
> Your body.

When you look at the most basic level, everything - the nonliving world, your body, and all of life – everything is made up of atoms. This is scientific fact. And what do we know about atoms?

An atom has two regions: The first is the nucleus which is made up of positively charged particles called protons and neutral, uncharged particles called neutrons. The second is a larger cloud of negatively charged particles called electrons that orbit around the nucleus.

All atoms, making up living and non-living matter are constantly vibrating and in motion, and they follow a law that has never been and never will be broken. Energy is constantly present with every atom, scientific fact.

Pause, and ask this question: What is the source of energy that science has proven exists in all life and non-living material?

I did not truly seek the answer to this question until my early 40s. I had spent most of my life living like I was the center of the Universe, ego driven and in flight from God because of my fear of Him.

Here's a quick synopsis of what I believe today based on my own experience. You can take it or leave it, but before you make any snap judgments, just try this on for size:

Whether you believe Creation happened over six days, six million years, or in one big bang is irrelevant.

The name that you give to your Higher Power is irrelevant.

The only Power in this universe comes from One Power. There is no multiplicity. Even though religions around the world give God many different names, there can only be One Power, One Creator, One God.

Everything comes from a Universal Creative Energy. And here is the amazing fact I was ignorant to: Each one of us is an individual expression of this Power.

Here is proof: If I took one drop of water from the ocean, it would still contain ALL the same properties as the entire ocean. This is fact.

The only difference? Volume.

What is the difference between a spark and a bolt of lightning?

Volume.

The exact same fact is true for each and every one of us. We are all an individual expression of our Creator, the only difference being in volume. God is alive inside every atom of our being. God is alive inside every atom of Creation.

Take note that I said we are all an individual expression of God, our Creator. I did not say that we are all gods. There can only be One Power, just like there can only be one answer for the mathematical equation of 1 + 1. The answer can only be 2. There is no other.

It does not matter what you call this Power - God, Power, Creative Energy, The Universe, Creative Intelligence, Life Force – there is only one God.

The good news is that God desires for all of us to be happy, joyous and free. Because we are made in the image and likeness of our Creator, we have been given the power to create with our thought.

Our purpose is to advance Creation using the talents we have been given in full partnership with the Infinite Intelligence living inside us.

The walls we construct out of fear lock out this Power within us. We worry and make accusations about other faiths. Our ego-driven thinking creates a conception of God that is not true. The longer we hold this false conception in our minds the further we separate ourselves from the abundant supply of all things good.

When we come to believe that all truths withstand observation, then we give ourselves the freedom from judging what others believe.

We leave the job to them, individually, to observe what they believe. And we can know that if they do observe and question their thoughts, they will find their Truth.

So, consider your relationship with God, Source, The Divine, Creation in the same way. If this Universal Power is a part of us and lives within us, then Universal Knowledge is always available to us.

The Creative Force does not trick us, bring misfortune, or seek to condemn us. Instead, what I define as God has made everything good abundantly available to us — what's not good comes from our own manifestation. We simply need to realize our true relationship with God to remove and conquer all fear.

Our conception of God is the foundation of our relationship with Him.

I lived over 30 years with a conception of God that kept me from trusting Him. My former conception of God grew to where it terrified me, and guess who helped develop this terrifying conception? My ego.

Through the use of the skills I learned and have shared with you, I came to a point where I asked myself if my conception of God was helping me or hurting me.

I spent several weeks with this question, and when observation clearly showed my conception was not helping me, the door was opened to ask more questions.

Why do I have this conception?

Who created this conception?

I observed how my fear of God had evolved. I looked at where I had placed blame on people, places, and institutions where I didn't think life was fair. I observed my anger with God and how I blamed God for setting me up to fail.

I asked myself if it was possible to change my conception of God. This concept of changing my conception of God was not new to me when I asked this. I had heard it many times before, but my fear of God had kept me from ever honestly asking the question to myself.

What I observed was that I had a choice. I could keep my current conception and continue to live in fear, or I could change my conception and see what happened. Facing the prospect of changing my conception, I was filled with ego-driven doubt. I battled these doubts for several weeks without much progress.

173

I was standing in my bedroom when out of nowhere the thought came to me, "Maybe, you should forgive yourself." I paused. Forgiving myself had been suggested to me before, but it never made sense. "How can you forgive yourself? That doesn't make sense," is what I would think or say.

But all of a sudden, the idea of me forgiving myself was front and center. If I had not been active asking myself questions, I would have quickly dismissed this opportunity.

So, I asked myself, "Can I forgive me?"

I didn't feel that I couldn't.

"What would I forgive myself for? How would I do it?"

I paced around my bedroom for a few minutes, asking these questions silently in my mind and made my way into the bathroom where I was standing in front of a mirror.

I moved closer to the mirror, resting my hands on the counter below and looked at myself. I remembered looking into this same mirror before many times, saying, "F*** you!"

I wondered why had I said that to myself before?

"Have I been hating myself?"

I looked into the mirror questioning if I had been hating myself. I started to feel sad, disappointed, angry.

"You, stupid son-of-a-bitch! Jesus!"

Unaware, I immediately went from the practice of observing my thoughts to judging them.

I began pacing again, beating myself up for hating myself. I could not have been thinking more insanely.

174

Then, out of the blue I thought the words, "Don't judge."

I paused and said, "Don't judge," and I started to chuckle.

I laughed out loud. "Don't judge," I said out loud again, laughing more. I realized that right on the very verge of change, I had allowed my ego to knock me off course.

I walked back into the bathroom and looked into the mirror. I stood there silent for about 30 seconds, looking into my eyes.

"I forgive you."

Saying this while looking into my reflection in the mirror felt awkward. Not much happened, and I didn't feel any different. So, I said it again.

"I forgive you."

I started to feel a bit more relaxed.

"I forgive you."

I smiled.

"I forgive you. I love you."

I started laughing out loud again, looking at myself saying, "I forgive you. I love you," over and over.

I realized that God had not been judging me; I had been my judge all along. I had created every false conception about myself and God.

It was in that very moment that I gave myself permission to change my conception of God.

My false conception of God was a force who was condemning, judging, punishing, up high on a mountaintop and completely out of reach. My new conception has evolved to one who is a loving, non-judging, cooperative force, with the desire for me to experience an abundance of happiness, health, and wealth.

You may have heard the expression, "God is either for us or against us." My conception is there is no possibility for God to be against us because God lives inside every atom of our being. God cannot destroy God, and therefore, God will not destroy me or you.

How do we come to believe anything? We only believe when we create and accept the conception of that thing. Whether our conceptions are created by strong, outside influences like family, celebrities, or leaders – we all individually accept and live by our conceptions.

We are individually 100% responsible for our conception of God, Source, The Divine. The definitions, observations, cultures, and religions outside you provide data and influence to create your conception, but nothing more. You are the sole acceptor of your conception of God.

If your God isn't working for you, maybe it's time to observe your conception.

CHAPTER SUMMARY

Fear, anxiety, and depression are our own creation. It is easier to be afraid than it is to consciously think. This is why so many of us stay trapped by fear. We don't actively try to conquer it.

My greatest fear was God.

Many of us were presented with the idea of God as an all-judging, condemning force that was looking for any reason to punish us.

I bought into this idea early that God would punish me severely if I messed up, so what did I do? I messed up! That's what humans do! We make mistakes and perfection is ultimately impossible, but we've adopted this false belief that we are supposed to be perfect.

It's pretty much crazy thinking.

I learned that God lives inside me, and His knowledge and power are available to me always. Knowing this newer conception, I see that God is for me. God is for all of us.

God is good and so am I.

TRAINING EXERCISE

For today, start to ask yourself what your definition of a power greater than you is…

Then, ask yourself what it would feel like if you had a force that was unconditionally loving and abundantly granting of good in your life. How would that feel?

GO DEEPER

Take some time just to be with yourself. Find a mirror you can look straight into. Smile at yourself. Say, "I love you."

If you are feeling a tightness in your stomach after reading this, that's ok. I experienced the same thing. The truth is that I used to hate myself. I would look in the mirror often and say, "F*** you."

If you're not able to tell yourself, "I love you," start with, "I forgive you," but don't just run into your bathroom and say it. Only do it when you can be completely honest with yourself. You'll know if you are being honest by how you are feeling. ⚘

*Your calm mind
is the ultimate
weapon against your
challenges. So relax.*

Bryant McGill

 CHAPTER 20

REALIZING THE BENEFITS OF THINKING BETTER THOUGHTS

I remember planting a bean seed inside a styrofoam cup in my second-grade science class. My classmates and I all had one that we cared for daily. We would add a little water, and then place our cup close to the window for the soil to be warmed by the sunlight.

Not a single classmate of mine poked their finger into the cup to see if the bean plant was starting to grow. We believed our teacher when she told us that if we did this, the plant would die. I, along with the rest of my classmates, did not want to be the one who's plant did not grow so I left it alone. We all followed the teacher's instructions, and we were all able to realize the positive effect of the experiment.

Was it hard to wait for the plant to start growing? Yes, and there were some of us, including myself, who became very impatient about it. There were a few classmates who had plants start coming through the soil before anyone else. This was torture. Why was my plant not growing? Was there something wrong with my seed? Did I not water it enough?

My teacher assured me everything would be fine. As much as I wanted that plant to show up, I had no choice but to wait. Picking through the soil to check its progress could potentially cause serious damage, and possibly even destroy the plant. Within a few days my plant, along with the rest of my classmates' plants, did exactly what they were programmed to do, grow into healthy bean plants.

This simple experiment from my second-grade science class illustrates how to acquire the things you desire in your life.

If your world is without, it is but a reflection of your world within. Your thought creates the conditions your mind images. Science has proven that your brain does not know the difference between what it sees in its environment with your eyes and what it remembers.

The hardest work in the world is keeping before your mind's eye the image of all you want to be.

Think abundance, feel abundance, believe abundance, see abundance and you will find that as you think and feel, believe, and see...abundance will manifest itself in your daily life.

You know that if you plant a seed in the right environment and water it, the seed will sprout and grow into whatever kind of plant it is. What part in this process do you have other than planting the seed and watering it? The answer is ZERO.

Everything other than planting and watering happens between the seed and the soil. If you want the seed to sprout and grow into a plant, you have to let the seed and soil work together without your interference.

Nature has given us some of the very best examples of how to be successful. Planting a seed in soil is one of my absolute favorites. When it comes to the subject of success, you have to allow your creative seeds to germinate and grow inside your subconscious mind.

The Creative Force behind the soil, nutrients, water, and seed that produces the plant is the same Creative Force that has always been and always will be available to you, God.

The thoughts you create penetrate your subconscious mind, which communicates with the Superconscious Mind. The Superconscious Mind has many names - Infinite Intelligence, Universal Mind, The Source, Divine Mind, One Mind, Infinite Wisdom, Mother Nature, God.

You were born with the power of thought. Every thought you have is a thing that creates the world around you because every thought is transmitted to the Superconscious Mind by your subconscious mind.

Your subconscious mind is subjective. It does not judge your thinking.

The subconscious mind is where all your personal experiences, emotions, beliefs, thoughts, and ideas are stored and can be accessed.

Your subconscious mind allows you to function on autopilot for many things in your life. You can go for months or even years without riding a bike and still be able to. This is because your subconscious mind has stored the knowledge of how to ride a bike in your mind; it's just a matter of accessing the stored knowledge.

If you do not keep your subconscious mind's eye on what you desire, you risk functioning on autopilot with doubt.

If your world is without, it is truly a reflection of the world within you because you are storing images of lack and failure in your subconscious mind that are being transmitted to the Superconscious Mind.

The Superconscious Mind does not judge the thoughts transmitted to it by your subconscious mind. If your focus is on what you don't have, you will continue to have experiences in your life that demonstrate what you don't have.

These are the thoughts you are planting and storing in your subconscious mind. These thoughts are all the Superconscious Mind has to work with for you. The Superconscious Mind cannot guess what you want.

Ego-driven thinking is the poison of this world. Allowing our egos control of our consciousness feeds our subconscious mind negative instructions which are then transmitted to the Superconscious Mind.

This is why we started with persistence. If you lack persistence, you will not be active in monitoring the thoughts you are feeding your subconscious mind.

Persistence is the tool used to make all the tools for thinking a better thought work –

> Knowing your ego and how it operates

181

Monitoring your feelings

Relaxing and recharging

Recognizing success in your life

Living with gratitude, free of all resentment

Practicing forgiveness

Removing negativity and worry

Not needing to be perfect or worry about what others think

Ending self-hate and letting pain go

And, removing fear by changing our conception of God, Infinite Intelligence, the Superconscious Mind to one full of love, faith, collaboration, and trust.

You can become a master of all these tools, but only if you do not quit.

It's quite possible that your subconscious mind today is full of doubts. The way to correct this is by changing your thoughts of fear and failure to thoughts of gratitude and success. You CAN reprogram your subconscious mind by only thinking thoughts of gratitude, success, happiness, health, and wealth.

You can remove all fear and failure from your subconscious, but it comes at a price.

The price is everlasting persistence in using the tools you have been given to only think thoughts of abundance, happiness, health, wealth, success, life, love, and gratitude; seeing in your mind the world you desire as a reality, not the world without.

Thinking of a better experience as your reality when you are surrounded by what you do not like or want is the hardest work you will ever do. It may feel overwhelming, especially when you compare yourself to what the world defines as successful.

Don't waste your thoughts competing with others for what they have. Instead, observe the unlimited supply all around you. There are more trees, flowers, rocks, animals, and resources than can be counted. There is limitless supply. There is more than enough for all.

When beginning this process or starting over because you previously quit, it's best to start with something small and easily attainable, something you have relatable experience to. Every success is a stepping stone to a greater success. When you set yourself up for success, you can only be successful.

I believe most people fall short of realizing their ideas because they dig up their seeds. They look at their styrofoam cup and only see a plant not growing. They start to worry about it growing, become inpatient, dig up their seeds, and replace them with seeds of doubt and failure.

What is the best way to start or get back on track? Start with a small plant, a small desire.

Small, big, or massive – all success can be created by right thinking. The more you affirm the process works, the greater your confidence and proficiency grows.

Start with something easily attainable. It is best to think of something you have experience of receiving previously so that there is absolutely no doubt it is possible for you to attain possession of it.

1. Be perfectly clear about exactly what you desire.
2. Ask yourself what the next right step is to receive it.
3. Know with undeniable faith that you DO receive it.
4. Express sincere gratitude in advance of receiving it, like you already have what you desire in your possession.
5. Believe, see, and feel the feelings of experiencing the reception of your desire. See yourself actually experiencing what you desire in the present moment.
6. Take action. When the opportunity to move toward your desire presents itself, ACT.
7. Recognize when you do receive it.
8. Express sincere gratitude for receiving what you desire.

Here's something easily attainable you can start with to test the process:

Create the desire of receiving a cup of coffee from Starbucks. It doesn't matter if you drink coffee or not. The point is to come into possession of a Starbucks coffee by creating this specific desire.

Remember, the idea of starting with a small object, like this cup of coffee from Starbucks, is for you to build the confidence you need for bigger and better things.

> Decide and be perfectly clear in your mind that you desire a cup of coffee from Starbucks. Close your eyes and see a white cup with the green Starbucks logo being handed to you. Feel yourself smiling and appreciating the friendly gesture of someone giving you this cup of Starbucks coffee without you asking for it.

> Visualize and feel the warmth of the cup as you accept and hold it in your hands. See the cup as you raise it to your mouth, continue to feel the warmth, and smell the aroma of the coffee you are about to drink.

> Taste and feel the warm coffee - from your lips, to your mouth, throat, and stomach.

You can create this entire visualization and experience in less than a minute. Do it at least twice a day, and don't be surprised when a cup of Starbucks coffee shows up within the next couple of weeks or sooner.

Wouldn't it be nice for you to state what you wanted, and for it to all come together, perfectly as you envisioned it with the least amount of effort? If you will start practicing this drill daily, with persistence, you will start to believe that it is actually possible to attain this talent.

Remember to start with things you have the belief are attainable and grow from there. Don't start with things you have no relatable experience to; this gives your ego more ammunition to create doubt.

Be specific and exact about what you desire. If I gave you a message in an envelope where all the sentences had been cut up into individual letters, you would have great difficulty decoding the message.

Your subconscious mind is not capable of decoding messages. Know exactly what you desire so it can be perfectly transmitted to the Superconscious Mind.

This is why I strongly suggest you start with something very small, like a friend buying you coffee from Starbucks. This is easy to see happening. It is small and specific, and you probably have a good idea of what a cup of Starbucks coffee looks, smells, tastes, and feels like.

Your subconscious mind acts on specific beliefs you have. If you doubt you can receive a cup of Starbucks coffee, your subconscious mind acts on doubt. Your subconscious mind accepts the belief that you do not think a cup of Starbucks is possible, and your mind is closed off to the possibility, missing opportunities to receive the coffee when they come.

You can take your cup of coffee and grow it into a free lunch, an unexpected $100 bill, and then to greater, and greater, and greater things. But start where you have relatable experience.

If the largest check you have ever received in your life was $5,000, it will be much harder for you to be successful with this exercise by desiring to receive a $5,000,000 check in a week. Even though it is entirely possible, you have no relatable experience anywhere close to receiving $5,000,000. In this example, your closest experience is receiving only $5,000.

The safer move would be to desire a $10,000 check. This is much more believable if the largest check you had previously received was $5,000. Start with relatable experience and grow from there.

What if you "try" and fail? What then? Ask yourself at what point of the process you allowed your ego to take control away, creating doubt. Observe the answer and do not judge yourself.

Be grateful that you discovered where you got off track and realize this discovery as a success. Persist and continue to work again and again until you experience success.

If you fail, it is only because you have not removed the possibility of failure from your thoughts.

Allow it to happen.

A good example of how this works happened to me on a flight from Phoenix to El Paso with my video producer, Ron. During the flight, I had nothing better to do than to think, which gave me an excellent opportunity to upgrade my day.

I visualized getting off the plane easily, picking up our luggage with no delay, and being offered a nice upgrade on our rental car for a more enjoyable 350-mile drive the next day.

By the time we landed and deplaned, I forgot that I had changed how I wanted my day to unfold.

The walk to get our bags was easy. There was no line at the rental car counter, but there was a problem. There was no record of our reservation, which created another problem. We couldn't rent a car for a one-way trip.

I kept my cool, but it was difficult. I told myself it would all work out, and visualized being home. The rental car agent soon found two cars available for a one-way rental.

What car did we receive? A BMW SUV at the same rental rate of the Nissan Rogue our original reservation was for, a pretty nice upgrade!

I started to take my shoes off in my hotel room, and that's when I realized what had happened. I had completely forgotten about re-creating my day on the airplane when I was standing in front of the rental car agent. Everything worked out exactly the way I desired it to be, but even better. I couldn't keep myself from laughing once I had realized what happened.

This is a really cool part I want you to get. I re-created my day, and then I simply allowed it to happen. I didn't pick out what car I wanted. I just decided I wanted an upgrade, and then I stepped out of the way and let it unfold in the most perfect way, never doubting.

Forgetting my intention was exactly what I needed. I needed to get out of the way for it to happen. Create your desire, turn it over to your subconscious mind, and get out of the way.

Now, let's really have some fun. Remember in the last chapter when the concept of taking one drop of water from the ocean was presented to you? The only difference between the drop and the entire ocean being volume?

Then God said, "Let Us make man in Our image, after Our likeness" - Genesis 1:27

Is it possible that being created in the image and likeness of God is similar to taking a drop of water from the ocean, the only difference in creative power being in volume?

"And if we are children, then we are heirs: heirs of God and co-heirs with Christ" – Romans 8:17

We are told we are made in the image and likeness of God. We are told that we are heirs of God and co-heirs with Christ, and what do we do? We squander it. We hide the talents we are given, creating a belief that we are not worthy.

You are a direct expression of God, The Father, The Universal Creator of All.

Allowing it to happen is the most perfect display of your faith possible because it is Creative Intelligence, God, the Father in all of us Who does the work.

Knowing what to do in your life can be simplified to this general description. We were created by The Great Creator. Our job here is to continue to create, to continue to advance God's creation.

Any good thought or idea we can create to advance God's creation has the potential full Power of God behind it. The only force that can stop it is the limitation we set in our mind, our lack of faith.

Have faith. Allow it to happen. Allow God to be the Power behind all your thinking.

Consider this scenario:

If a son asked his father for a new bicycle, and the father had more than enough resources to give his son the bicycle, he would not give his son a piece of glass, would he?

No. He would buy him the best bicycle he could, and add a helmet, knee and elbow pads, and accessories to go with it. The father would give his son the very best possible.

Your Father in Heaven desires for you to have the very best in your life. The only limitation of what your Father can give to you is created by you.

Think A Better Thought™. Believe. Receive. Allow it to happen.

CHAPTER SUMMARY

When you dine at a restaurant this is the typical process before you receive your food:

You are seated by the hostess and given a menu.

Your waiter arrives at your table and takes your drink order. Your waiter may also inform you of that evening's specials.

You survey the menu, and inside your head you imagine the experience of dining on one or many different options.

You give your order to the waiter.

188

Then what do you do? You may visit, enjoy drinks, or maybe watch something playing on TV. Are you doing anything to prepare your meal? No. You are allowing the meal to be prepared for you. The only involvement you have in preparing your meal is deciding what you want.

Have you ever thought about having a menu where you could choose what experiences you would like to enjoy?

TRAINING EXERCISE

It helps to have a relatable experience for this exercise so that you already believe it is possible. As you think of the experience for this exercise, resist the temptation to "go big." There will be plenty of time to do that later.

Think of something you enjoy that you may not have had in a while. Make sure you think of something that you have previously received.

It could be a meal, a friend's company, or flowers at work.

Now decide on how you would like to receive it again.

Know that you will receive it.

Do not question for one moment the fact that you will receive it.

Every day visualize and believe that this thing you want is coming into your life. This is important. If at any time you have a doubt, you will be hitting the breaks and throwing all your momentum in reverse.

The probability of you having a doubt about receiving it is high when you first begin to practice this exercise. Know this. You are not the first person to have a doubt about receiving something you are visualizing, even something small like a friend buying you coffee.

When this happens, do not judge yourself. Instead, realize the success you have made in recognizing a negative thought and being able to correct it, and re-focus your thoughts on the end result. The end result is the actual experience of receiving the thing you are visualizing.

Allow it to come into your life.

Recognize when this happens, and when it does express sincere gratitude for receiving it.

Bonus Exercise:

Meditate on your relationship with your Higher Power. Ask yourself if you see yourself as a direct expression of God.

GO DEEPER

If the answer to, "Can I see myself as a direct expression of God?" is, "No," then you are really being honest with yourself. We are programmed with the word, no, early in childhood. It is with the best intention by our parents. They start telling us, "No," to keep us safe.

This word continues to grow in use and many times we create the habit of telling ourselves, "No," internally. If you have created this habit, you need to be patient with yourself. You may slip and tell yourself, "No," many times before you finally break through.

The difference in slipping now and before is that you will be aware of when you do it. Be persistent in starting right back where you left off.

This exercise requires discipline, patience, and persistence. It also requires you to be very forgiving of yourself. Eliminate all doubt. Believe. Doubting is negative. Be disciplined enough to withstand all doubt. You can.

Learn to say, "Yes," to yourself. ⚘

Relax and enjoy
your coffee.

Shane Boring

YOUR GRATITUDE LIST

_____

_____

_____

_____

_____

_____

_____

_____

_____

_____

_____

_____

_____

_____

_____

_____

_____

_____

_____

_____

_____

_____

_____

_____

_____

_____

_____

_____

_____

_____

_____

_____

_____

_____

_____

_____

_____

_____

_____

_____

_____

_____

_____

_____

_____

_____

_____

_____

_____

_____

_____

_____

_____

_____

_____

_____

_____

_____

_____

ACKNOWLEDGEMENTS

Writing this book has been a true learning experience, and it would have been a much greater challenge without the priceless support of great people.

Thank you to my wife, Dedee. You are the most amazing person I have ever known, and your unconditional love is beyond description. You patiently supported me in every aspect, giving your honest feedback that helped take this book from an outline of ideas to a tool that can be understood and applied by the masses. Every page of this book is rich with your story, love, and support.

Thank you to my children, Bryce, Blake, Anna, and Max. Not only did you endure your dad learning to think in a new way, but you helped me time and again by listening to my ideas, giving me your own ideas, and constantly showing me support by asking how the book was going. I love you all.

Thank you to Suzanne Tappe, who spent hundreds, possibly thousands of hours working on research, organizing content, proofing, and publishing Think A Better Thought™.

Thank you to my team (former and current) at SDB Creative Group, Dedee, Bryce, Zane, Kayla, Lindsay, and Amy who have supported this work with enthusiasm, great ideas, and exceptional creative used to promote Think A Better Thought™.

Thank you to Ron McWilliams for your input and work with video production.

Thank you to Judy Tseui, who encouraged me to tell my story more and taught me how to communicate more effectively through writing.

Thank you to Mark McDonald, who took the time to listen and guide a first-time author. You may think your involvement was minimal, but those short conversations helped solidify the commitment to create a quality work.

Thank you to the wonderful people listed below for taking the time to read Think A Better Thought™ in advance and offering their invaluable feedback to help make the book the very best possible. Whether you read the entire book, met with me on it, or just showed interest, your support is deeply appreciated.

Keri Zamora	Colin Tepfer
Ronnie Stewart	Alyse Bolda
Amy Bray	Scholley Bubenik
Nolan Schattel	Douglas Green
Sharon Schattel	Richard Sanger
Noe Ramirez	Bryce Boring
Joni Lownik	Dedee Boring
Misty Stewart	Elizabeth Boring
Mary Butler	Kim Guarino
Susan Barbour	Paige Murphy
Amy Prause	Ingrid Pagliaro
Greg Wassberg	Noe Ramirez
Brian Plumer	Andy Karr
Elizabeth Wood	Michael Ang

And, thank you to all the teachers, known and unknown, who have given the world and me the gift of their knowledge. ⚘

Made in the
USA
Lexington, KY